INSIGHT GUIDES

LONDON

POCKET GUIDE

PLAN & BOOK
YOUR TAILOR-MADE TRIP

BRAZIL CHILE ECUADOR

TAILOR-MADE TRIPS & UNIQUE EXPERIENCES CREATED BY LOCAL TRAVEL EXPERTS AT INSIGHTGUIDES.COM/HOLIDAYS

Insight Guides has been inspiring travellers with high-quality travel content for over 45 years. As well as our popular guidebooks, we now offer the opportunity to book tailor-made private trips completely personalised to your needs and interests. By connecting with one of our local experts, you will directly benefit from their expertise and local know-how, helping you create memories that will last a lifetime.

HOW INSIGHTGUIDES.COM/HOLIDAYS WORKS

STEP 1

Pick your dream destination and submit an enquiry, or modify an existing itinerary if you prefer.

STEP 2

Fill in a short form, sharing details of your travel plans and preferences with a local expert.

STEP 3

Your local expert will create your personalised itinerary, which you can amend until you are completely satisfied.

STEP 4

Book securely online. Pack your bags and enjoy your holiday! Your local expert will be available to answer questions during your trip.

BENEFITS OF PLANNING & BOOKING AT INSIGHTGUIDES.COM/HOLIDAYS

PLANNED BY LOCAL EXPERTS

The Insight Guides local experts are hand-picked, based on their experience in the travel industry and their impeccable standards of customer service.

SAVE TIME & MONEY

When a local expert plans your trip, you save time and money when you book, even during high season. You won't be charged for using a credit card either.

TAILOR-MADE TRIPS

Book with Insight Guides, and you will be in complete control of the planning process, from the initial selections to amending your final itinerary.

BOOK & TRAVEL STRESS-FREE

Enjoy stress-free travel when you use the Insight Guides secure online booking platform. All bookings come with a money-back guarantee.

WHAT OTHER TRAVELLERS THINK ABOUT TRIPS BOOKED AT INSIGHTGUIDES.COM/HOLIDAYS

Trip to Vietnam

The organization was superb, the drivers professional, and accommodation quite comfortable. I was well taken care of! My thanks to your colleagues who helped make my trip to Vietnam such a great experience. My only regret is that I couldn't spend more time in the country.

Heather   ★★★★★

DON'T MISS OUT BOOK NOW AT
INSIGHTGUIDES.COM/HOLIDAYS

TOP 10 ATTRACTIONS

TOWER OF LONDON
Where many a historic head has rolled.
See page 65.

HARRODS
London's most famous corner shop, known for its exquisite Art Nouveau food hall. See page 74.

TATE MODERN
Feted for its architecture and its excellent collection of modern and contemporary art. See page 54.

BIG BEN
The clocktower (officially now the Queen Elizabeth Tower) dominates the Palace of Westminster, home of the Parliament. See page 30.

NATIONAL GALLERY
Located in Trafalgar Square, it houses Britain's finest collection of European art. See page 26.

THE BRITISH MUSEUM
Situated in Bloomsbury, it houses artefacts from antiquity to the present. See page 45.

COVENT GARDEN
Named after its market, it's a lively area for shopping and street performance. See page 36.

ST PAUL'S CATHEDRAL
Sir Christopher Wren's masterpiece is the jewel of the City. See page 62.

BUCKINGHAM PALACE
Witness age-old traditions at the Queen's London residence. See page 40.

THE LONDON EYE
Take a ride for spectacular views over London. See page 51.

A PERFECT DAY

9.30am

Breakfast
Get the day off to a good start with a full English breakfast, either at your hotel or from the superb breakfast menu at The Wolseley on Piccadilly.

2.00pm

Covent Garden
Head south via Seven Dials towards Covent Garden, where retail therapy options abound. Meander along Neal Street, lined with fashion-forward boutiques, to Long Acre, where upmarket chain stores offer a more high-street experience.

10.00am

Royal Park
Take a morning stroll in one of London's leafy central parks – St James's, Green or Hyde. Catch the Changing of the Guard on the hour from 11am Mon–Fri (10am Sun) at Horse Guards Parade or at 11am at Buckingham Palace (only every other day Aug–Apr).

12 noon

Culture fix
Take the Piccadilly line to Russell Square and walk to the British Museum, a treasure trove of world artefacts. Among the highlights are the Elgin Marbles and the stunning Egyptian collection. If you're hungry, grab a snack at the café in the magnificent Great Court.

3.30pm

Art and cake
Ten minutes' walk away is the National Portrait Gallery, where you can check out some famous royal portraits, then settle into the rooftop Portrait Restaurant, with its spectacular views of Westminster, for an extended traditional afternoon tea.

IN **LONDON**

6.30pm

Southbank sunset
Just north of Westminster Bridge is the London Eye, a great way to get a bird's eye view of London at sunset, or the city lights at night. If you're ready for another rest stop, Gordon's Wine Bar, the oldest in London, is just across the Hungerford Bridge at 47 Villiers Street.

10.30pm

On the town
Time for a nightcap. Stay on Brick Lane for eclectic tunes and a relaxed vibe at 93 Feet East; alternatively, get a cab, the no. 67 bus or walk up to Shoreditch, which is teeming with great bars. Start at hip but friendly Hoxton Square Bar & Kitchen, then party the rest of the night away at Cargo (83 Rivington Street), a trusted favourite.

5.00pm

Westminster
Take a walk through Trafalgar Square and south along Whitehall to Parliament Square, where you will find Westminster Abbey, the Houses of Parliament and Big Ben. Then head across the Thames on Westminster Bridge to the South Bank.

8.30pm

East End dining
Get the District line from Embankment to Aldgate East, a short walk from vibrant Brick Lane. Try Tayyabs on nearby Fieldgate Street for a cheap, authentic curry. Alternatively, get off at Cannon Street, walk past St Paul's Cathedral and enjoy great views as you have a drink or dine at Madison on the rooftop of the One New Change shopping centre.

CONTENTS

⬤ INTRODUCTION 10

🏛 A BRIEF HISTORY 14

🎡 WHERE TO GO 25

Westminster 25
Trafalgar Square 25, Whitehall 28, The Houses of Parliament 29,
Westminster Abbey 30, Tate Britain 31

The West End 32
Piccadilly Circus 32, Oxford Street 34, Soho and Chinatown 34,
Leicester Square 36, Covent Garden 36, Somerset House 38, The
Embankment 39

Buckingham Palace and Mayfair 40
Buckingham Palace and the Parks 40, St James's 41, Mayfair 43

Bloomsbury and Marylebone 45
The British Museum 45, King's Cross and St Pancras 47, The
Regent's Park 48, Marylebone 49

The South Bank 50
County Hall 51, The London Eye 51, The Southbank Centre 52,
Around Waterloo 53, Around Gabriel's Wharf 53, Tate
Modern 54, The Millennium Bridge 55, Shakespeare's Globe 55,
Southwark 56, Tower Bridge 59, Butlers Wharf 60

The City 61
Legal London 61, St Paul's Cathedral 62, The Barbican 63, The
Financial City 64, The Tower of London 65

Kensington and Chelsea 67
Hyde Park and Kensington Gardens 67, Kensington 70, South
Kensington 70, Knightsbridge 74, Chelsea 75

North London 76
Islington 77, Camden 77, Hampstead and Highgate 78

East London 79
Spitalfields and Whitechapel 79, Hoxton 80, Docklands 81,
Stratford 81

Southeast London 82
Greenwich 82, Dulwich 85

Southwest London 85
Wimbledon, Richmond and Kew 85, Hampton Court 87

☺ WHAT TO DO _____ 89

😊 EATING OUT _____ 102

◎ A–Z TRAVEL TIPS _____ 118

🛏 RECOMMENDED HOTELS _____ 134

🌐 INDEX _____ 140

◉ FEATURES

London cabbies _____ 13
Blue plaques _____ 19
Historical Landmarks _____ 23
Shepherd Market _____ 44
Literary Bloomsbury _____ 46
Portobello Road Market _____ 73
2012 Olympics _____ 99
Calendar of Events _____ 101
Eating and drinking hours _____ 104

INTRODUCTION

William Shakespeare could have been referring to London, his adopted hometown, when he wrote, 'Age cannot wither her, nor custom stale her infinite variety.' London is steeped in history, architectural wealth, cultural capital and international political, economic and religious influence. It is a cosmopolitan place with an open attitude to diversity. You can pick through a cornucopia of international cuisine, while the city's famous pubs, bars and entertainment suit all tastes.

For a tourist, central London is compact and fun to explore by bus, or Boris bike. Yet London is not without its problems. The basic cost of living – from food prices to travel and rent – is high compared with that in many other capitals and, certainly, other cities in the UK. Despite the expensive public transport system, the Tube remains overcrowded and there are few days when every line works without delays. House prices and rents increase annually in the centre, meaning ever-longer commutes for London's workforce.

The 'Big Smoke' has its major pollution concerns too, owing to traffic congestion, although this is certainly nothing new – in 1819 the poet Percy Bysshe Shelley wrote 'Hell is a city much like London, A populous and smoky city.' The 'congestion charge' scheme, which taxes anyone driving through a central zone (Mon–Fri 7am–6pm), has reduced casual traffic on the city's streets during peak hours and raised funds for the public-transport system; yet local businesses bemoan the reduction in footfall, matched with ever-increasing rents.

But the city still manages to maintain its allure; a combination of history and opportunity, culture and excess. London is often said to be France's sixth biggest city, due to the size of its French expat community. It is both melting pot and mould for its globalised community. After decades of decline, London's population has increased since the mid-1980s to its present 8.8 million. More than one in three residents is from a minority ethnic group, and around 300 languages are spoken. Service industries such as catering and hospitals rely heavily on immigrant labour.

Cyclists at Hyde Park Corner

THE CLIMATE

The climate in London is mild, with the warming effects of the city itself keeping off the worst of the cold in winter, with January temperatures averaging 5°C (41°F). Temperatures in the summer average 23°C (73°F), but they can soar to well over 30°C (86°F), causing the city to become stiflingly hot.

Temperatures can fluctuate considerably from day to day, and surprise showers catch people unawares all year round. This unpredictability has its plus side – Brits love to talk about the weather. Unsuspecting visitors should come prepared with water-proof clothing and an umbrella. Layers are also sensible.

AN ORGANIC CITY

Take your time in London because you have no chance of seeing it all. Apart from the city's vast size, its long and venerable past is sometimes hidden from view. Over the centuries the ripples

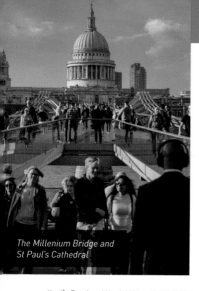

The Millenium Bridge and
St Paul's Cathedral

of history have repeatedly destroyed parts of the city, and the subsequent rebuilding has resulted in a blend of architectural styles. To make the most of it, pick your battles wisely and master just a few key areas or sights.

Modern London is the product of continual upheaval. The plague of 1665 claimed the lives of ~and in 1666 the Great Fire destroyed much of the city (incredibly only six people died). During World War II, 29,000 Londoners were killed; 80 percent of buildings in the financial district were damaged and a third were destroyed.

Yet each destruction bore its own seeds of change. The streets in the old City of London were so dark that shopkeepers positioned mirrors outside their windows to reflect light inside. The bombing of World War II eventually provided the opportunity for widening and lightening; slums disappeared, and street crime declined.

A CITY IN VOGUE

Every now and then the city becomes brazenly fashionable – the Swinging London of the 1960s, for instance, or 'the coolest place on the planet', as *Newsweek* dubbed it in the 1990s. After nearly half a decade in the shadows of the 2008 recession, the city's mood began to lift. 2012 was a bumper year, with the Queen's

Jubilee and the London Olympics both putting the city firmly back on the international map. The city's economy continues to grow more than anywhere else in the UK. London's success places it in stark contrast with other UK cities, a disparity which came to the fore in 2016 when London bucked the national trend with 59.9 percent of voters opting to remain in the EU referendum.

London is a patchy, unplanned city, where you never know what you are going to find around the next corner. You may discover the pomp of State occasions, the grind of a weekend carnival, a narrow medieval alley, or the surprise of the blue plaques, which highlight the former homes of everyone from Benjamin Franklin to Jimi Hendrix. Certainly, there is enough to keep even the most demanding of visitors and locals busy, or as Dr Samuel Johnson famously declared, 'when a man is tired of London, he is tired of life; for there is in London all that life can afford.'

⊙ LONDON CABBIES

Perhaps the closest most visitors get to meeting a true Londoner is when they catch a black cab. Taxi drivers, or cabbies, are experts on the city, and are essential to its life, coursing through its veins in their black cells. About 25,000 drivers work in London, driving either rented or owned vehicles. The classic cab, the Austin FX4, was launched in 1958, and still going strong in its updated incarnation. Prospective black cab drivers spend up to four years studying London's roads, remembering a total of 320 routes, as well as 25,000 streets and 20,000 places of interest. After passing a written exam and oral tests, drivers get their licence. Cabbies may not always know what they're talking about, but they always know where they're going.

A BRIEF HISTORY

Although Julius Caesar landed in England in 56 and 55BC, he came, he saw and he left without leaving any trace of a settlement. It remained for the Emperor Claudius and his Roman legions to conquer the island in AD43 and build what was believed to be the first bridge over the Thames – roughly on the site of today's London Bridge – establishing the trade port of Londinium.

The Romans built roads, forts, temples, villas, a basilica, forum and a huge amphitheatre (excavated near the Guildhall in 1988) for a population of around 50,000 living in the area now known as the City. The Roman's rule was often challenged, and so they erected vast stone walls around their city.

SAXONS AND NORMANS

In 410, as the Roman Empire declined, London's legions were recalled to Rome. The walled area of Londinium became a ghost town, buried under silt and grass, and avoided by subsequent invaders. Eventually, the Saxons came over the North Sea to build Lundenwic, and, after a brief return to paganism, the seeds of Christianity – sown in the later-Roman period – sprouted in London again. St Ethelbert, the first Christian king, dedicated a small church to St Paul here; it has since been destroyed and rebuilt five times.

The Saxon kings were constantly at battle with Viking and Danish invaders, and when the Danes conquered and put King Canute on the throne in 1016, London unseated Winchester as the capital of the kingdom. In the 1040s Westminster Abbey was built by Edward the Confessor, a pious though ineffectual king. When the Norman army of William the Conqueror was victorious at the Battle of Hastings in 1066, William began the tradition of being crowned at the Abbey. He respected London's wealth and commercial energy, and shrewdly forged a relationship with the Church and citizenry that benefited all concerned. He also instigated work on the Tower of London.

The Tower of London

FEUDAL ENGLAND

During the early Middle Ages London's influence grew, while the kings of England were diverted by wars in France and Crusades to the Holy Land. Under Henry I, London's citizens won the right to choose their own magistrates, and during the reign of the absentee king, Richard the Lionheart (1189–1199), the elective office of Mayor (later Lord Mayor) was created.

England's medieval monarchs did not enjoy blind loyalty from London's citizens, whose strong trade and craft guilds, which still exist, created a self-determinism and power that often resulted in rebellions. The Palace of Westminster became the seat of government, and one of the reputed reasons for its riverside site was that a mob could not surround it.

By 1340 London's population hit around 50,000, but in 1348 disaster struck. The Black Death swept across Eurasia, killing 75 million. Details of the horrors in London are scarce, and there are no accurate figures on the final death toll; however, it is estimated that almost half of London's population was hit.

Portrait of Elizabeth I

London was still little bigger than it had been in Roman times, but this was about to change. The decision by Henry VIII to break relations with Rome gave birth to the Church of England and also added property in the form of seized monastery lands, such as Covent Garden (once a convent garden).

THE ELIZABETHAN ERA

Between the death of Henry VIII in 1547 and the coronation of his daughter Elizabeth I in 1558, religious persecutions and political intrigues drained the kingdom's coffers and influence. However, under the 45-year reign of Elizabeth, England rose to unforeseen heights, with London the epicentre of a mighty kingdom. The defeat of the Spanish Armada in 1588 signalled the dawn of empire, as the British Navy took to the seas in search of riches. The prosperity of Elizabeth's reign was marked by the blossoming of English literature, with Shakespeare the jewel in the crown of literati including Christopher Marlowe and Ben Jonson.

REVOLUTION AND RESTORATION

In marked contrast, Elizabeth's successors are remembered principally for their failures. In 1605 James I narrowly escaped assassination in the abortive Gunpowder Plot – Guy Fawkes was discovered in the cellars of the Houses of Parliament about to light the fuse that would have blown up the king at the opening of Parliament on 5 November. This act is still commemorated annually around the country on 'Bonfire Night'.

James I's son, Charles I, was even less popular. By attempting to dissolve Parliament, the feckless king plunged the country into Civil War. In 1642 the Royalists ('Cavaliers'), supported by the aristocracy, went into battle against the Parliamentary forces. The 'Roundheads', named after their 'pudding-basin' hairstyle, were backed by the tradesmen and Puritans, and led by Oliver Cromwell. The Royalists were defeated at Naseby, Northamptonshire, in 1645. In 1649 Charles I was found guilty of treason and beheaded. Cromwell assumed power and abolished the monarchy, and for a short period Britain was a republic. In 1653 Cromwell declared himself Lord Protector, remaining so until his death in 1658. However, by 1660 the country was disenchanted with the dreary dictatorship of Puritan rule, and the monarchy was restored under Charles II.

DISASTERS AND RECOVERY

The relaxation of the Puritan mores was not long enjoyed. In 1665 a terrible plague stalked London, killing an estimated 110,000 people. Death, disease and decay turned the city into a madhouse, in which piles of bodies were left in its streets, until taken away by cart to be buried.

In 1666 disaster struck again, in the form of the Great Fire. About 80 percent of the old City burnt down, and 100,000 people were made homeless. Incredibly, due to a speedy evacuation, the number of recorded deaths is in single figures. Sir Christopher Wren was appointed joint head of a commission to oversee the rebuilding of the city, and though his grand schemes were never fully realised, he made a huge contribution to the new London, including rebuilding St Paul's. The Monument (see page 65) is his memorial to the fire.

Stained glass portrait of Dr Samuel Johnson, Fleet Street

The final great confrontation between king and parliament involved James II, brother of Charles II. A fervent Catholic, James attacked the Church of England and disregarded the laws of the land. However, the people of England had no stomach for cutting off another royal head, and in 1688 James fled the country. The so-called Glorious (peaceful) Revolution ushered in William of Orange and Mary II to the throne, establishing a stable constitutional monarchy. Under William and Mary, a royal retreat was established at Kensington Palace.

GEORGIAN GREATNESS

In the 18th and early 19th centuries, London was the capital of a world power. In the coffeehouses of the City and West End, great men of letters such as Alexander Pope and Samuel Johnson held forth. Handel was court composer to King George I, and Kew Gardens and the British Museum were opened to the public. But there was a dark side to London – slums grew up south of the river and in the East End, and crime was rife.

Overseas the Empire was burgeoning, until a tax dispute caused a rift between Britain and the American colonies. This escalated into a war over independence, and, to the astonishment of George III, the colonists won. By the end of the 18th century, Britain was threatened with Napoleonic invasion, but

Nelson disposed of the French fleet at the Battle of Trafalgar in 1805. Some 10 years later, the Duke of Wellington put an end to Napoleon's ambitions at the Battle of Waterloo.

THE VICTORIAN EMPIRE

The accession of the 18-year-old Queen Victoria in 1837 gave title to England's most expansive age. The Empire building that was started in Elizabeth I's day was taken to new heights in the 19th century. Ships filled with the bounty of the colonies not only brought goods with which to trade at the East End docks, they also drew in new languages, cultures and citizens who helped to shape the cosmopolitan capital.

In 1851 Victorian progress was feted at the Great Exhibition, held in Hyde Park in Joseph Paxton's vast, specially designed iron-and-glass Crystal Palace. Transported south of the Thames to Sydenham in 1852, the edifice gave its name to a new Victorian suburb, Crystal Palace; sadly, the grandiose building itself burned down in 1936.

⊘ BLUE PLAQUES

In 1867 a blue ceramic plaque was erected on the front of 24 Holles Street by the Royal Society of Arts (RA) to commemorate Lord Byron, who was born there. Across London there are now over 900 such plaques, each giving facts about the figure concerned. For a plaque to be awarded, the person being remembered must have been dead for at least 20 years and the building must survive in a form that he or she would have recognised. The range has so far been dominated by male politicians and artists, although English Heritage have pledged to honour more women in coming years.

With the money taken at the Great Exhibition, Prince Albert, Queen Victoria's consort, realised his ambition: a centre of learning in the form of the Victoria and Albert Museum. This was followed by the Queen's tributes to her husband, the Royal Albert Hall and Royal Albert Memorial.

However, while the rich grew fat and complacent, the poor were increasingly wretched, and the pen of Charles Dickens pricked many a middle-class conscience with his portrayal of the misery and hopelessness of the souls condemned to poverty in this 'prosperous' city. London was growing rapidly, and by 1861 it had 3 million inhabitants. The East End slums expanded to house the newcomers pouring into the city looking for work. The boundaries of London were pushed well out into the countryside with the development of public transport. Newly invented omnibuses, trains and, in 1863, the world's first underground railway, created a new breed of London citizen; the commuter.

TWO WORLD WARS

In 1915 the German Zeppelins dropped the first bombs on London, and World War I left London's young generation grossly depleted. This was a mere foretaste of what was to come 25 years later – Hitler's Blitzkrieg rained bombs down on London between September 1940 and May 1941, during which the city experienced 57 consecutive nights of bombing. In June 1944 the rockets known as 'doodlebugs' were launched, battering London until March 1945. By the end of the war London's death toll was over 30,000, with 3.5 million homes damaged or destroyed. Through it all strode Winston Churchill, the indomitable spirit of wartime Britain.

POST-WAR BOOM AND LABOUR'S LEGACY

Life in post-war Britain was spent clearing rubble and living frugally. By the 1950s, however, spirits were lifting and the arts were feted again in the capital in 1951 at the Festival of Britain. The greatest legacy of the festival was the South Bank Centre, an arts complex built south of the Thames. London enjoyed a huge boom of popularity into the 1960s, when a stream of rock and rollers, artists and fashion designers put London firmly on the map. The explosion of anarchic punk culture in the 1970s was followed by the rampant materialism of Thatcherism and Conservative rule from 1979 to 1997.

Most Londoners welcomed Labour's landslide victory in the 1997 election under Tony Blair. As areas of the city including Bankside were regenerated, the capital was celebrated in the press as 'the coolest place on the planet'. The Labour government decided to restore a measure of self-government to the capital by creating an elected mayor. Changes introduced by the first mayor, Ken Livingstone, included the 'congestion charge' aimed at tackling traffic jams and pollution.

By 2005, Labour's ongoing popularity had slipped significantly, thanks in no small part to Blair's controversial decision to go to war in Iraq. Despite this, the government was re-elected. On 7 July 2005 London suffered a severe blow when, in Britain's first suicide-bombing, terrorists hit Underground and bus targets in the capital, killing 52 people and injuring around 700.

CONSERVATISM, AUSTERITY MEASURES AND BREXIT

In the 2008 mayoral election, Livingstone was ousted by Conservative politician Boris Johnson (re-elected in 2012). In the 2010 general election, Labour was defeated again; the new government was a Conservative/Liberal Democrat coalition, who introduced a programme of austerity measures.

In 2011 the wedding of Prince William to Catherine Middleton relieved Britain's sodden mood. This was followed, in 2012, by the Queen's Jubilee and the Olympic and Paralympic Games, which boosted the UK economy by £9.9 billion. 2013 saw the birth of Prince George, the first child of Prince William, the Duke of Cambridge, and Catherine, the Duchess of Cambridge. In April 2015 the Duchess gave birth to her second child, Princess Charlotte. In 2016, Sadiq Khan succeeded Boris Johnson as mayor and London celebrated the Queen's 90th birthday. Former Home Secretary Theresa May became Britain's second female Prime Minister following the EU referendum in which the electorate narrowly voted leave ('Brexit').

On 22 March 2017, London was left reeling when a terrorist drove into pedestrians on Westminster Bridge, killing four, before fatally stabbing a policeman outside the Houses of Parliament; two months later terrorists killed eight and injured 48 at Borough Market. In between the shocking attacks, May triggered Article 50, the two-year negotiation period for agreeing a divorce settlement with the EU. The Conservative Party lost its majority in a snap election, but May quickly agreed a deal with Northern Ireland party, the Democratic Unionist Party (DUP), to have its support in key votes. 2018 and 2019 brought some light relief with a flurry of royal news: the Duke and Duchess of Cambridge celebrated the birth of Prince Louis on 23 April, while Prince Harry and Meghan Markle got married at a star-studded event in Windsor Castle in May. A year later, Meghan gave birth to Prince Archie.

HISTORICAL LANDMARKS

AD 43 Emperor Claudius establishes the trade port of Londinium.

61 Boudicca sacks the city but is defeated, and London is rebuilt.

c.200 City wall built. London becomes the capital of Britannia Superior.

410 Romans withdraw to defend Rome. London falls into decline.

884 London becomes the capital under Alfred the Great.

1348–9 Black Death wipes out 50 percent of London's population.

1534 Henry VIII declares himself head of the Church of England.

1605 Guy Fawkes attempts to blow up James I and Parliament.

1642–9 Civil war between Royalists and Roundheads.

1665 Plague hits London again, killing around 110,000 citizens.

1666 Great Fire of London.

1837–1901 Victorian Empire-building and the Industrial Revolution.

1851 Great Exhibition in Joseph Paxton's Crystal Palace in Hyde Park.

1863 London Underground opens its first line, the Metropolitan line.

1888 Serial murderer Jack the Ripper strikes in Whitechapel.

1914–18 World War I. Zeppelins bomb London.

1922 The BBC transmits its first radio programmes.

1939–45 World War II. London is heavily bombed.

1951 Festival of Britain. South Bank Centre built adjacent to Waterloo.

1980s Margaret Thatcher years. Several IRA bombs hit London.

1996 Shakespeare's Globe opens on Bankside.

2000 London celebrates the millennium. Ken Livingstone elected Mayor.

2005 Suicide bombers kill 52 and injure approximately 700 people.

2008 Boris Johnson elected Mayor of London. Global Financial Crisis.

2012 Queen's Jubilee. Olympics held in London. Johnson re-elected.

2013 The Duchess of Cambridge gives birth to Prince George.

2015 Princess Charlotte is born. Conservative Party win the general election.

2016 Sadiq Khan elected Mayor. UK narrowly votes leave in EU referendum.

2017 Five people killed in Westminster terrorist attack. UK triggers Article 50. Eight die in Borough Market terror attack.

2018–19 Prince Louis is born. Prince Harry and Meghan Markle get married; their first child, Prince Archie, is born a year later.

Buckingham Palace

WHERE TO GO

There are as many opinions on the best way to tour London as there are places to see. First-time visitors may find a ride on an open-top bus (see page 125) helpful in getting their bearings round the city centre. Once you've identified which area to explore, it's best to pound the streets, and seeing the city this way enables you to trace the city's development through its varied architecture.

WESTMINSTER

The centre of official London, Westminster today is very different from its 11th-century origins as a marshy island where Edward the Confessor built a church, 'West Minster', and a palace. Nowadays, it is home to the UK Parliament and London's *grand place*, Trafalgar Square.

TRAFALGAR SQUARE

Named after the naval battle that took place in 1805 off Cape Trafalgar, southwest Spain – at which Admiral Lord Nelson defeated Napoleon – **Trafalgar Square ❶** is as good a place as any to start a tour of London. Once criticised as little more than a glorified, polluted roundabout, the north side has been completely pedestrianised and the square has become the focus for many of London's top cultural events, festivals and political protests.

Towering high above the square is the 170ft (52-metre) **Nelson's Column**, topped by a statue of Britain's most famous maritime hero. Adjacent are the stone lions by Sir Edwin Landseer that provide a popular spot for tourists after photo opportunities. Look out for the fourth plinth, in the northwest corner of the square, used to showcase temporary works of art by contemporary artists. Past

The National Gallery

commissions have gone to Antony Gormley, Rachel Whiteread, Marc Quinn and David Shrigley.

National Gallery

Dominating the north side of the square is the **National Gallery** (www. nationalgallery.org.uk; daily 10am–6pm, Fri until 9pm; free except some special exhibitions), which houses Britain's finest collection of European art dating from 1250 to 1900. The gallery was founded in 1824, when a private collection of 38 paintings was acquired by the British Government for £57,000 and exhibited in the owner's house at 100 Pall Mall. As the collection grew, a new building to accommodate it was planned. William Wilkins' grand neoclassical building opened in 1838 in the then-recently created Trafalgar Square. The Sainsbury Wing, to the west of Wilkins' building, was added in 1991, designed by the American architect Robert Venturi in witty postmodern style. The two buildings are bridged by a circular link, and the pleasant paved area between them offers a short-cut to Leicester Square (see page 36).

The collection, which contains over 2,000 works, is divided into four sections. The Sainsbury Wing houses paintings from 1250 to 1500, including Jan van Eyck's *Arnolfini Portrait*, Botticelli's *Venus and Mars* and Leonardo da Vinci's *The Virgin of the Rocks*. The West Wing contains paintings from 1500 to 1600, including Titian's *Bacchus and Ariadne* and Holbein the

Younger's *The Ambassadors*. In the North Wing you can admire paintings from 1600 to 1700 including Velázquez's *Rokeby Venus*, Rembrandt's *Self Portrait*, and Van Dyck's *Equestrian Portrait of Charles I*. The East Wing covers art from 1700 to early 20th century and includes works by the English painters Constable and Gainsborough and Impressionists such as Monet, Van Gogh, Cézanne and Renoir.

National Portrait Gallery

Adjoining the National Gallery, the **National Portrait Gallery** (2 St Martin's Place; www.npg.org.uk; daily 10am–6pm, Fri until 9pm; free except special exhibitions) was founded in 1856 as a 'Gallery of the Portraits of the most eminent persons in British History'. Additions to the collection have always been determined by the status of the sitter and historical importance of the portrait, not by their quality as works of art. Highlights include Holbein's drawing of Henry VII and his son Henry VIII, a life-like portrait of Queen Elizabeth I, in brocade and pearls, and self-portraits of Hogarth, Gainsborough and Reynolds.

St-Martin-in-the-Fields

At the northeast corner of the square is the church of **St Martin-in-the-Fields** (www.stmartin-in-the-fields.org; Mon–Fri 8.30am–6pm, Sat–Sun 9am–6pm, with exceptions; free). This is the oldest building in Trafalgar Square, built in 1724 by a Scottish architect, James Gibbs, when the venue was literally in fields outside the city. This is the parish church of the royal family and the royal box can be seen on the left of the altar. Nell Gwynne, mistress of Charles II, is one of several famous people buried here. The church is renowned for its classical and jazz concerts, held at lunchtimes (usually free) and in the evenings. The crypt houses a brass-rubbing centre and a pleasant café.

Changing the Guard

WHITEHALL

The avenue of government buildings that runs south from Trafalgar Square to Parliament Square is named after Henry VIII's Palace of Whitehall, which once stood on this spot, but burned down in 1698. The first major place of interest on the west side of the street is the Palladian-style **Horse Guards ❷**, built between 1751–3 on the site where the main gateway to the Palace of Whitehall once stood. Two mounted Life Guards duly maintain their traditional sentry posts Mon–Sat between 11am and 4pm each day (Sun from 10am), changing every hour (www.royal.gov.uk). The archway in the building leads through to the huge Horse Guards Parade ground, which adjoins St James's Park (see page 41).

Opposite Horse Guards is **Banqueting House** (www.hrp.org.uk; daily 10am–5pm), one of England's first Renaissance buildings, and the only surviving part of the Palace of Whitehall. It was built in 1619 by Inigo Jones for James I and inspired by Jones's hero the 16th-century Italian master Palladio. Its major interior feature is a splendid ceiling by Rubens, commissioned by Charles I. Ironically, Charles was later beheaded in front of this very building.

A little further down on the right hand side is **10 Downing Street** (www.gov.uk/government/organisations/prime-ministers-office-10-downing-street), office and residence of the prime minister since 1735. Barriers at the end of the street prevent the public from viewing the famous doorway.

Just south of here in the middle of the street is the **Cenotaph**, a memorial designed by Sir Edwyn Lutyens commemorating the dead of both world wars. Continuing south towards Parliament Square you pass the imposing headquarters of the Foreign Office and the Treasury. At the far end of King Charles Street, which runs between them, are the **Churchill War Rooms** (www.iwm.org.uk; daily 9.30am–6pm), where you can explore Churchill's underground World War II command post and a museum about his life and work.

THE HOUSES OF PARLIAMENT

The neo-Gothic Victorian triumph on the banks of the Thames is the **Palace of Westminster ❸**, better known as the Houses of Parliament. Guided tours (75 mins) are available on Saturdays throughout the year and weekdays during the summer recess (www.parliament.uk; 9.15am–4.30pm). At other times of year (Oct–July) UK residents can contact their MP to request a free tour or free tickets to watch a parliamentary debate (Prime Minister's Question Time is on Wednesdays from noon) and overseas residents can obtain tickets for debates by queuing on the day.

The original palace was built for Edward the Confessor around 1065, and for 400 years it was a royal residence. However, the only medieval part of the palace remaining is Westminster Hall, built in 1099. In 1834, someone disposed of several ancient wooden tally-rods in the basement furnace, and the resulting conflagration consumed most of the building. Many considered it a blessing to be able to rebuild the draughty old edifice. The architect Sir Charles Barry was the driving force behind the new design, a 'great and beautiful monument to Victorian artifice', which was completed in 1860.

The neo-Gothic vision that is the Palace of Westminster

The most famous element of Barry's design is the clock tower housing **Big Ben** (UK residents can arrange a free tour by contacting their MP; no children under 11), a 13.5-ton bell, now officially called the Elizabeth Tower in honour of the Queen's 60-year reign. Its popular name is thought to commemorate Sir Benjamin Hall, Chief Commissioner of Works when the bell was cast in 1859; however, it may also have been named after a boxer of the day, Benjamin Caunt. Big Ben fell temporarily silent in 2017 due to major repair works on the tower, expected to last until 2021.

WESTMINSTER ABBEY

Facing the Houses of Parliament is **Westminster Abbey** ❹ (www.westminster-abbey.org; Mon–Tue, Thu–Fri 9.30am–3.30pm, Wed 9.30am–3.30pm & 4.30–6pm, Sat 9.30am–1pm, May–Aug until 3pm). Henry III built much of the abbey in the 13th century in early English Gothic-style, and it remained an important monastery until 1534 when Henry VIII dissolved the monasteries. After this, the abbey was still used as the royal church for coronations and burials, and all but two monarchs since William the Conqueror have been crowned here.

Beyond the nave, in the south transept, is **Poets' Corner**. Geoffrey Chaucer was the first poet to be buried here, in 1400.

Behind the sanctuary are ornate royal chapels and tombs. The **Tomb of the Unknown Warrior**, west of the nave, holds the body of a soldier brought from France after World War I.

In 2018, the abbey's medieval galleries, located 70ft (21m) above the nave, opened for the first time in 700 years. The Queen's Diamond Jubilee Galleries (Mon–Fri 10am–3pm, Sat: Sept–Apr 9.30am–12.30pm, May–Aug until 2.30pm) displays a collection of treasures, along with excellent views into the church and across Parliament Square.

Southwest of here, at the other end of Victoria Street, is London's Roman Catholic cathedral, the outlandish Italian-Byzantine style **Westminster Cathedral** (www.westminster-cathedral.org.uk; tower: Mon–Fri 9.30am–5pm, Sat–Sun 9.30am–6pm; free), which dates from the 19th century. There are fine views from the Viewing Gallery, perched 210ft (64-metres) up its distinctive striped tower.

TATE BRITAIN

About 15 minutes' walk south of Parliament Square, on the riverside near Vauxhall Bridge, is **Tate Britain ⑤** (www.tate.org.uk; daily 10am–6pm; free except some special exhibitions). The nearest tube station is Pimlico, from where the gallery is well signed.

Although somewhat eclipsed by its newer sister gallery, Tate Modern (see page 125), Tate Britain is still the main national gallery for British art, showcasing works from the 16th century to the present day. Some highlights of the collection include Hogarth

Dead poets

Literary figures buried in Poets' Corner include Alfred Tennyson, Ben Jonson (who is buried standing upright), Thomas Hardy, Charles Dickens, Robert Browning and Rudyard Kipling.

portraits, Constable's *Flatford Mill*, Millais's *Ophelia*, the pre-Raphaelite paintings of Dante Gabriel Rossetti, Stanley Spencer's *The Resurrection*, *Cookham*, Francis Bacon's *Study of a Dog* and David Hockney's *Mr and Mrs Clark and Percy*. Among the British 20th-century sculptors represented are Jacob Epstein, Barbara Hepworth and Henry Moore.

The Clore Gallery (an extension of the main building) was built in the 1980s to hold the Tate's huge and magnificent J.M.W. Turner collection, which includes 282 oil paintings and over 30,000 other works by the Covent Garden-born artist.

THE WEST END

Despite its misleading name, which reflects the fact that it is west of 'The City', the West End is actually London's central shopping and entertainment hub. It is a sprawling part of town, stretching from Oxford Street in the north, through Soho, Chinatown and Covent Garden, to the Thames-side Embankment in the south.

Though the area doesn't boast a lot of traditional 'sights', it is thronged with tourists and locals, day and night, as it is home to the city's greatest concentration of shops, theatres, restaurants, bars and clubs.

PICCADILLY CIRCUS

At the heart of the West End is bustling **Piccadilly Circus** ❻, whose illuminated advertisements first

The Tate Boat

If you're interested in visiting both Tate galleries, the Tate Boat runs all year round, every 40 minutes, between Tate Britain and Tate Modern during gallery opening hours, and also stops at the Embankment, near Westminster. Tickets are available from both galleries; advance tickets are valid for use all day.

The Shaftesbury Memorial Fountain
in Piccadilly Circus

appeared in 1890. Three years later, a memorial to the philan-
thropic Seventh Earl of Shaftesbury was erected in the circus,
topped by a statue of a winged figure, popularly known as 'Eros',
but actually a representation of Anteros, the Greek god of selfless
love. Nearby is Body Worlds London (www.bodyworlds.com; daily
9.30am–7pm, Fri–Sat until 9pm), the first permanent museum for
Gunther von Hagens' mildly macabre touring exhibition of plas-
tinated dead bodies, which offers a fascinating insight into the
anatomical workings of the human body.

Running northwest out of Piccadilly Circus is **Regent Street**,
designed by John Nash as a ceremonial route to link Carlton
House, the long-demolished Prince Regent's residence at
Piccadilly, with Regent's Park. Despite the Regency connections,
the elegant shop fronts disguise how young the street actually is – much of it was built in the 1920s, over 100 years after
Nash began work. The main section of Regent Street – between

Piccadilly Circus and Oxford Circus – is notable for its massive shops, including Arts and Crafts flagship store, Liberty, and the seven-floored Hamleys, the largest toyshop in the world.

OXFORD STREET

Bordered by Marble Arch to the west and the crossroads with Tottenham Court Road to the east, **Oxford Street ❼** is the busiest and most famous – although admittedly not the most glamorous – of London's shopping streets. The quality of establishments along its length varies wildly, from market stalls and discount stores selling Union Jack T-shirts, through branches of most of the major high-street chains, to top-class institutions such as Selfridges department store.

Named after the Earl of Oxford, who owned land north of here from the 16th century, the road was built as a main route out of the city and was intended to link the counties of Hampshire and Suffolk. From the 1760s it began to develop as an entertainment centre. The Pantheon (replaced by Marks & Spencer in 1937) housed fetes and concerts, and Jack Broughton's amphitheatre, on the corner of Hanwell Street and Oxford Street, was famed for its boxing bouts and tiger baiting. By the late 19th century, however, the street was becoming established as a place for retail therapy. Furniture store Waring & Gillow opened in 1906, while the department stores Selfridges and Debenham and Freebody (now Debenhams) – both of which have stayed loyal to the street – opened in 1909 and 1919 respectively.

SOHO AND CHINATOWN

Soho ❽, the area bordered by Regent Street, Oxford Street, Charing Cross Road and Shaftesbury Avenue, has long been the focal point of London's nightlife. Soho is characterised by narrow streets peppered with bars, cafés, restaurants, theatres, small shops and boutiques, though life has not always been so hectic here. Before the 1666 Great Fire of London, this area was open land where people came to hunt – the name 'Soho' is thought to derive from a hunting cry. After the fire, the area's open land was used for new housing and, in the late-17th and 18th centuries, it was inhabited by noblemen and eminent socialites.

Purchase-laden shoppers heading home from Oxford Street

However, by the 19th century, wealthy Londoners were moving out to Mayfair (see page 43), and Soho was taken over by the bohemian crowd. Its coffee houses and ale-houses soon became places for debate, founding a tradition that continues today in drinking clubs such as the Groucho Club. In the 20th century the area became increasingly cosmopolitan. By the 'swinging sixties', Soho's seedier side had come to the fore, and prostitution and the porn industry were rife. In 1972 the Soho Society was formed, and the group launched a campaign to clean up the area; by the early 1980s all sex shops had to be licensed.

The area is now known primarily as the focus of London's LGBTQ scene and for its excellent clubs, restaurants and bars. The main locations to check out include Old Compton Street, the area's main artery, and Soho Square, an unexpected green space that gets very crowded in summer. There's also an authentic outdoor fruit-and-vegetable market in Berwick Street and, in the west, pedestrianised Carnaby Street, which although not at the cutting edge as it was in its 60s heyday is still worth a look for its fashion boutiques.

At the southern edge of Soho is Shaftesbury Avenue, the heart of London's Theatreland. On the other side of the street is **Chinatown**, a tiny district that centres on Gerrard Street. Street names are subtitled in Chinese, and the tops of telephone boxes resemble mini pagodas.

LEICESTER SQUARE

South of Chinatown is **Leicester Square** ❾, which can be accessed via Leicester Place, home to the arthouse Prince Charles cinema and the French church Notre Dame de France. The expansive square is dominated by big cinema complexes, where many of the capital's blockbuster premieres take place, alongside chain restaurants and mainstream nightclubs.

COVENT GARDEN

With its pedestrianised cobbled streets, markets, opera house, shops, theatres, cafés and bars, **Covent Garden** ❿ is one of central London's most appealing areas. It has a lively atmosphere and attracts a mix of people including opera and theatregoers, street performers, shoppers and tourists.

The area owes its name to the fact that it was once pastureland belonging to the convent of Westminster Abbey. After the dissolution of the monasteries the land was given to the first Earl of Bedford, then in the late 1620s the Covent Garden that we see today took its form, when the fourth Earl commissioned Inigo Jones to design buildings 'fit for habitation'. Influenced by his studies of Palladian architecture in Italy, Jones created the main piazza, which consisted of St Paul's Church and three sides of terraced houses. Although the design found little favour with Jones's contemporaries, it attracted rich, aristocratic families.

However, Covent Garden's popularity as a chic residential area was short-lived. In 1670, Charles II granted a licence for flowers and vegetables to be sold here, and with the arrival of the market and the lower-class people it attracted, the area began a slow decline. By the late 18th century it was best known for coffee shops, prostitutes and brothels. The market was held here until 1974, when it moved to

A taste of China

its present site in Vauxhall, south London.

The central **Market Hall** was designed by Charles Fowler in 1831. Today it hosts a selection of small shops, various arts and crafts market stalls, several bars and restaurants and various spaces where buskers perform. Street entertainers also utilise the space in front of **St Paul's Church** (www.actorschurch.org; Mon–Fri 8.30am–5pm, Sat opening times vary – see website for details, Sun 9am–1pm; free) on the western side of the square. St Paul's is known as the 'actors' church', owing to its long association with the many theatres in the parish, and it contains memorials to Charlie Chaplin, Noel Coward, Vivien Leigh and Gracie Fields.

At the northeast corner of Covent Garden is the **Royal Opera House** (www.roh.org.uk), the third theatre to have stood on this site since 1732 (two previous buildings burnt down). The present one, which dates from 1946, was refurbished for the millennium at a cost of £120 million; facilities for the performers were improved, air-conditioning was introduced into the auditorium, and the glass **Floral Hall** (now known as the Paul Hamlyn Hall and a delightful place for coffee) was rebuilt next to the main house. Both opera and ballet are performed here.

Located in the southeast corner of the piazza, the **London Transport Museum** (www.ltmuseum.co.uk; daily 10am–6pm, ticket is valid for one year from purchase) utilises many interactive exhibits to trace the development of the city's buses, trams and tube since 1800, as well as exploring the future of public transport in the capital. It is an excellent place to take young children.

SOMERSET HOUSE

Just south of Covent Garden, parallel to the Thames, is the **Strand**, a road that links Westminster to the City along a route opened in Edward the Confessor's time. The church on an island at the eastern end of the Strand is **St Mary-le-Strand**. Built in 1724, it originally stood on the north side of the street, but, with the advent of the motorcar, the Strand was widened, and the church was left in odd isolation.

Opposite St Mary-le-Strand is **Somerset House** ⓫ (www.somerset house.org.uk; courtyard daily 7.30am–11pm, galleries Mon–Tue, Sat–Sun 10am–6pm, Wed–Fri 11am–8pm, last admission 1 hour before closing; free except special exhibitions), a grand example of neoclassicism, designed in the 18th century by Sir William Chambers. Located on the site of a 16th-century palace, Chambers' noble edifice was built to house government offices, including the Navy Board, and the three main learned societies of the United Kingdom: the Royal Academy of Arts, the Royal Society and the Society of Antiquaries. By the early 20th century the build-ing was mainly used as the headquarters of the Inland Revenue and the Registry of Births, Marriages and Deaths. In the 1970s it was decided to return it to public use – it is now home to an exhibition space dedicated to presenting contemporary arts in innovative ways. The central courtyard is a fabulous space, housing an ice-rink in winter and hosting live music performances and open-air cinema screenings in summer.

Also housed in the complex is the **Courtauld Institute of Art Gallery** (www.courtauld.ac.uk; daily 10am–6pm), a compact and impressive collection of Old Masters

There are plenty of refreshment options in the Market Hall

and Impressionist and Post-Impressionist works, including famous paintings by Manet, Cézanne, Degas, Monet, Renoir and Van Gogh. The gallery is closed for redevelopment and is expected to reopen in late 2020.

THE EMBANKMENT

Parallel to the Strand is the riverside Embankment, which is the site of London's oldest outdoor monument, **Cleopatra's Needle**. Cut from the quarries of Aswan (c.1475BC), the 68ft (21 metre) Egyptian obelisk is one of a pair (the other is in New York) and was given to the British Empire by the Turkish Viceroy of Egypt in 1819. It took 59 years for the British to move it from where it lay in the sand to its present position – it was intended to stand in front of the Houses of Parliament but the ground there was too unstable. It is said that the sphinxes at the base are facing in the wrong direction.

BUCKINGHAM PALACE AND MAYFAIR

West of Piccadilly Circus is the smartest part of central London. The area has consistently retained its social prestige since the building of its great estates began in the 1660s. With its Georgian residences, gentlemen's clubs and exclusive shops, it is synonymous with wealth. The area is divided in two by Piccadilly. To the north of this famous thoroughfare lies Mayfair, to the south St James's, the royal parks and Buckingham Palace.

BUCKINGHAM PALACE AND THE PARKS

The Queen's main London residence, **Buckingham Palace** ⑫ (www.royalcollection.org.uk; times vary, check website for details) was originally built in 1702 for the Duke of Buckingham, then bought by George III and enlarged for George IV by the architect John Nash. The main facade is a later addition – by Aston Webb in 1913. The Queen and Duke of Edinburgh occupy about 12 of the palace's 775 rooms, on the first floor of the north wing. If the Queen is in residence, the royal standard flies from the central flagpole.

The building was opened to the public in 1993 to help pay for the repairs to the fire-ravaged Windsor Castle, and now partly opens in summer/early autumn when the Queen is away, with some exclusive guided tours (around £85 per person) held in winter. The 19 State Rooms open to the public include the Dining Room, Music Room and Throne Room.

The Queen has one of the world's best private art collections, comprising about 9,000 works, including exceptional drawings by Leonardo da Vinci and royal portraits by Holbein and Van Dyck. A selection is on show in the **Queen's Gallery** (Buckingham Palace Road; www.royalcollection.org.uk; daily mid-Nov–mid-July 10am–5.30pm, mid-July–Sept 9.30am–5.30pm, last admission at 4.15pm).

Most people in the crowds outside Buckingham Palace come to see the **Changing the Guard** at 11am (daily May–July, alternate mornings Aug–Apr). The New Guard, which marches up from Wellington Barracks, meets the Old Guard in the forecourt of the palace, and they exchange symbolic keys to the accompaniment of regimental music.

North of the palace is **Green Park** ⓭, the smallest of the royal parks and the only one without flower beds – hence the name. The park was once a burial ground for lepers, and its lush grass is said to be a result of this.

Running east from Buckingham Palace is the Mall, the sweeping boulevard that edges **St James's Park** ⓮. The park is the oldest of the royal parks, built by Charles II, who had been exiled in France and wanted to recreate the formal gardens he had admired there. The bird sanctuary on Duck Island is now home to exotic waterfowl and pelicans (the legacy of a pair presented to Charles II by the Russian ambassador in 1665).

ST JAMES'S

St James's, the area north of the park, is the epitome of aristocratic London and the heart of clubland in the old-fashioned sense (gentlemen's clubs not nightclubs). In its 18th-century heyday it was an upper-class male bastion; nowadays, there

Looking along the Mall towards Buckingham Palace

St James's Palace, after which the area is named

are very few gentlemen's clubs left, but the district is still home to centuries-old wine merchants, milliners, shirtmakers (notably on Jermyn Street) and shoe-makers who cater for discerning masculine tastes.

St James's Palace (closed to the public), north of the Mall, was built as a hunting lodge in 1532 by Henry VIII. The palace was the official residence of the court before Buckingham Palace was first used for that purpose in 1837. It is now home to several members of the royal family, including the Princess Royal. Adjacent is Clarence House, the London residence of the Prince of Wales.

Also on the north side of the Mall, in Carlton Terrace, is the **Institute of Contemporary Arts**, or **ICA** (www.ica.art; institute Tue–Thu, Sun noon–11pm, Fri–Sat until midnight, galleries Tue–Sun noon–9pm; free except special exhibitions). In addition to the gallery spaces, where changing art exhibitions are held, the centre is home to a decent café/restaurant, a bar (comedy and other events are sometimes staged here), a theatre, a tiny bookshop and two cinema screens, where arthouse movies are shown.

Beside the ICA, on the route to the east end of elegant Pall Mall, is the **Duke of York's Column**, a memorial to George III's impecunious son, who was the Commander-in-Chief of the British Forces. The Duke died with debts of over £2 million, and the statue was paid for by withholding one day's pay from every officer and soldier. North of here is elegant **Pall Mall** where exclusive gentlemen's clubs mingle with the grand homes of royalty. Off the north side of Pall Mall is **St James's Square**, laid out by Henry Jermyn, the first Earl of St Alban in about 1660.

Parallel to Pall Mall, running west from Piccadilly Circus towards Hyde Park Corner, is **Piccadilly**. The road is one of the main routes in and out of the West End, and its name comes from the 'pickadills', or ruffs, worn by the dandies who frequented the area in the 1600s. At 197 Piccadilly is **St James's Church** (www.sjp. org.uk), designed in 1684 by Sir Christopher Wren. It has a craft market and coffee house and holds excellent classical concerts.

A few doors down is **Fortnum & Mason** ⓯ (www.fortnum andmason.com), London's most glamorous grocers and purveyor of goods to the Queen for over 300 years. Enjoy the quintessential (if pricey) afternoon tea here or further along the road at **The Ritz** (www.theritzlondon.com; reservations essential; dress smartly).

MAYFAIR

To the north of Piccadilly is **Mayfair**, one of the classiest areas in the capital and the most expensive place to land on the English Monopoly board. The second most expensive, Park Lane, bounds the area to the west, while Oxford Street marks Mayfair's northern side. The district takes its name from a riotous 17th-century fair and still contains dozens of narrow alleys and cut-throughs that give the visitor a flavour of 17th-century London. It was at this time that the area was first transformed from a swampy plague pit where highwaymen preyed on passers-by to the fashionable place to be seen, and where Regency bucks such as Beau Brummell chaperoned respectable ladies on their morning strolls.

On Piccadilly is the 17th-century Burlington House, home of the **Royal Academy of Arts** ⓰, or RA, (www.royalacademy.org.

uk; daily 10am–6pm, Fri until 10pm), entered through a huge arch and across a large courtyard and known for high-profile temporary exhibitions. Its less-known permanent collection includes Michelangelo's *Taddei Tondo*, Constable's *The Leaping Horse* and Gainsborough's *A Romantic Landscape with Sheep at a Spring*. Diploma work, submitted by Academicians on election to membership, includes Walter Sickert's *Santa Maria delle Salute*, Richard Eurich's *The Mariner's Return* and David Hockney's A Closer *Grand Canyon*. Built as part of a renovation project to mark its 250th anniversary, Weston Bridge links Burlington House to additional gallery space and a lecture theatre in Burlington Gardens.

Alongside the RA is the **Burlington Arcade**, built in 1815 and one of the oldest, most elegant of the capital's covered shopping promenades. Beadles patrol this Regency promenade. In their top hats and livery, they ensure good behaviour, with 'no undue whistling, humming or hurrying'.

Mayfair's other upmarket retail environments include the bespoke suits of **Savile Row**, the commercial art galleries of **Cork Street**, auction houses Sotheby's and Bonhams, and **Old Bond Street** and **New Bond Street**, both of which are famous for their proliferation of designer flagship stores. Off New Bond Street is

⊙ SHEPHERD MARKET

The pedestrianised enclave off Mayfair's Curzon Street (or via Clarges Street or Half Moon Street from Piccadilly) was named after Edward Shepherd, who built the area in the mid-18th century. In the 17th century, the annual 15-day 'May Fair' was held here, hence the name of the whole area. Shepherd Market is now a great place to relax, with bars, Victorian pubs and restaurants aplenty, many of which have pavement tables.

Brook Street where at No. 25 is Handel & Hendrix in London (www.handelhendrix.org; Mon–Sat 11am–6pm), where the composer of *The Messiah* lived from 1723 until his death in 1759. Next door, much later (1968–9) lived a very different musician – Jimi Hendrix – whose upper floor flat opened to the public in 2016.

Mayfair's Burlington Arcade

BLOOMSBURY AND MARYLEBONE

Despite their central location, both Marylebone and Bloomsbury are surprisingly genteel. Marylebone High Street and Marylebone Lane enjoy a village atmosphere, and many of London's top doctors have surgeries around Harley Street and Wimpole Street. East of Tottenham Court Road is Bloomsbury, London's literary heart and home to the British Museum, British Library and much of the University of London.

THE BRITISH MUSEUM

The **British Museum** ⓱ (www.britishmuseum.org; Great Russell Street; daily 10am–5.30pm, Fri until 8.30pm; free), opened in 1759, is the nation's greatest treasure house, with items from Neolithic antiquities to 20th-century manuscripts. The main entrance is via the steel-and-glass-roofed Great Court, Europe's largest covered space, in the middle of which is the grand former main reading room, now an information centre. Behind the famous Athenian frontage are the 5th-century BC Elgin Marbles 'rescued' by Lord Elgin from the Parthenon in Athens in 1801, and the linguist's codebook, the Rosetta Stone, the key that unlocked the mysteries of ancient Egyptian hieroglyphics. There are excellent Assyrian, Egyptian and Roman artefacts in the main museum, including the world's richest collection of Egyptian mummies and funerary art, the exquisite 1st-century Roman Portland Vase and the Nereid Monument, an elaborate Turkish tomb dating from 380BC. Also worth seeing are the Assyrian Lion Hunt Reliefs, which display the ultimate sport of kings.

Though a world museum, it is guardian of the great British treasures, too, including the Sutton Hoo trove from a burial ship of an Anglo-Saxon king, the 7th-century Lindisfarne Gospels and Lindow man, a Briton killed 2,000 years ago and preserved in a peat bog.

Continuing north towards King's Cross divert east to 48 Doughty Street and the **Charles Dickens Museum** (www.

⊙ LITERARY BLOOMSBURY

In the early 20th century Bloomsbury was home to Virginia Woolf, Vanessa Bell, Duncan Grant, Dora Carrington, Roger Fry and Queen Victoria's biographer, Lytton Strachey, known collectively as the 'Bloomsbury set'. Although their inclinations spread across painting, philosophy and writing, their connection was to challenge the conventions of the day. At that time publishing was a major industry in the area, with publishers including the Bloomsbury set's own Hogarth Press. Many imprints have since moved to cheaper premises, however, as have most of the area's second-hand bookstores.

dickensmuseum.com; Tue–Sun 10am–5pm, last admission 1 hour before closing). The author lived here from 1837–9 while writing *Nicholas Nickleby* and *Oliver Twist*. It is the only one of his London homes still standing, and exhibits all manner of memorabilia: his letters, manuscripts, desk, locks of his hair and even his lemon squeezer.

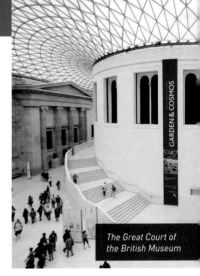

The Great Court of the British Museum

KING'S CROSS AND ST PANCRAS

The area around King's Cross and St Pancras stations is well on the way to complete regeneration, with the fully overhauled **St Pancras International** itself one of the architectural and retail highlights of the area. The immense Victorian Gothic red-brick and glass edifice is London's Eurostar terminus, while the adjacent St Pancras hotel has been restored to its former glory. Just behind Granary Square, where 1,000 illuminated fountains shoot up daily between 8am and 7pm, lies the Coal Drops Yard development, a high-end shopping and dining space.

The **British Library** (www.bl.uk; 96 Euston Road; Mon–Thu 9.30am–8pm, Fri 9.30am–6pm, Sat 9.30am–5pm, Sun 11am–5pm; free) used to be housed in the British Museum, but as the museum collection grew, it was decided to move the 9 million books, including a Gutenberg Bible, the Magna Carta and original texts by Shakespeare and Dickens. Galleries in

One of the taller inhabitants of London Zoo

the current premises, near St Pancras, display some of the library's treasures, ranging from a 3rd-century biblical manuscript to original copies of Beatles' lyrics. The library hosts changing literary-themed exhibitions, many of which are free, and has five places to eat and drink.

West of here on Euston Road is the **Wellcome Collection** (www.wellcomecollection.org; galleries Tue–Sat 10am–6pm, Thu until 10pm, Sun 11am–6pm; library Mon–Fri 10am–6pm, Thu until 8pm, Sat 10am–4pm; free), which showcases an eclectic mix of art, books and medical artefacts, including a replica shrunken head, a chastity belt and Napoleon Bonaparte's toothbrush.

THE REGENT'S PARK

Further west still is **The Regent's Park** ⓲, an elegant 470-acre (190-hectare) space surrounded by smart Regency terraces. Within the park are formal gardens, an open-air theatre where plays, including Shakespeare, are staged in summer, and a boating lake. Regent's Canal runs through the north of the park. Also at the northern end of the park is **London Zoo** (www.zsl.org/zsl-london-zoo; daily late Mar–early Sept 10am–6pm, early Sept–late Oct 10am–5pm, late Oct–mid-Feb 10am–4pm, late Feb–late March 10am–5.30pm), which is home to more than 660 species of animal. There are lions, tigers, gorillas and hippos, with many breeding programmes for endangered species, including Tiger Territory and the Land of the Lions, which is home to one male and three female endangered Asiatic lions. The zoo is expensive, but discount offers, including 2-for-1 entrance with a train ticket, can help bring down the price.

Northwest of Regent's Park is **Lord's Cricket Ground** (www.lords.org; tours hourly on the hour daily Jan–Feb 11am–2pm, Mar, Nov–Dec 10am–2pm, Apr–Oct 10am–3pm), the ancestral home of cricket. To visit the ground, the portrait-lined Long Room through which players walk on their way to the field, and the memorabilia-packed MCC Museum, you have to take a 100-minute tour, which runs most days except on important match days.

MARYLEBONE

South of the Regent's Park is **Madame Tussauds** (www.madametussauds.co.uk/london/en; hours vary – see website for details – but generally Mon–Fri 9.30am–5.30pm, Sat–Sun 9am–6pm, spring/summer school holidays 9am–7pm). The waxworks museum is home to thousands of effigies of various celebrities from royals to filmstars to Marvel superheroes, made with glass-fibre bodies and wax heads. It was founded in 1835 by Marie Tussaud, who prepared death masks of famous victims of the guillotine during the French Revolution. Those gory beginnings are echoed in the Chamber of Horrors.

Nearby at 221b Baker Street is the **Sherlock Holmes Museum** (www.sherlock-holmes.co.uk; daily 9.30am–6pm). It pays tribute to Sir Arthur Conan Doyle's fictitious sleuth by creating an imaginative evocation of the Victorian detective's apartment.

Other cultural attractions in Marylebone include the Art Nouveau **Wigmore Hall** (36 Wigmore Street; www.wigmore-hall.

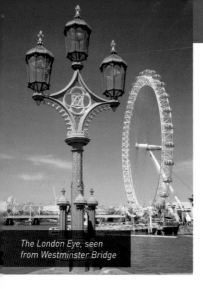

The London Eye, seen from Westminster Bridge

org.uk), a notable venue for chamber music, and the **Wallace Collection** ⑲ (Hertford House, Manchester Square; www.wallacecollection.org; daily 10am–5pm; free except for some special exhibitions), a fine private collection of 17th- and 18th-century English and European paintings, porcelain and furniture, elegantly displayed in an 18th-century mansion. Highlights include Franz Hals' The Laughing Cavalier, Jean-Honoré Fragonard's The Swing and furniture attributed to master cabinetmaker André-Charles Boulle.

THE SOUTH BANK

The area south of the Thames, from County Hall (opposite Westminster) to Southwark, further east, is an historic part of London. The first bridge across the Thames was built by the Romans near London Bridge, and the community around it developed as an alternative to the City, since it lay beyond the City's jurisdiction. In Shakespeare's day this was a place for showing unlicensed plays and setting up brothels, and it retained its reputation as an area of vice well into the 19th century.

In the late 20th century the area was transformed into a vibrant cultural centre; warehouses were renovated and converted into expensive flats, and the Underground's Jubilee Line extension improved access. Highlights of the area now include the London Eye, South Bank Centre, Tate Modern and Shakespeare's Globe. Further east, the capital's (and Western Europe's) tallest building, The Shard, has led regeneration of the London Bridge area. Located beside London Bridge station, at 1,016ft (310m) tall, it contains several restaurants, the 5-star Shangri-La hotel, offices and a viewing gallery (see page 58).

COUNTY HALL

Facing the Houses of Parliament is the neoclassical **County Hall**, built from 1909–22 and once the seat of the Greater London Council, which ran London until an unsympathetic Thatcher government abolished it in 1986. It now houses two hotels, several restaurants and various family attractions. The **Sea Life London Aquarium** (www.visitsealife.com/london; Mon–Fri, Sun 10am–6pm, Sat 9.30am–7pm; last admission 1 hour before closing) contains thousands of specimens representing around 500 species of fish in 15 themed zones. The **London Dungeon** (www.thedungeons.com/london/en; Mon–Fri, Sun 10am–5pm, Thu 11am–5pm, Sat 10am–6pm) is a theme park of gore, focussing on London's bloody history. Shrek's Adventure (www.shreksadventure.com; daily 10am–4pm, with exceptions) is a walk- and ride-through experience that allows you to mingle with characters from the famous movie.

THE LONDON EYE

Towering over County Hall is the **London Eye** ⓴ (www.londoneye.com; Jan–Mar and Sept–Dec Mon–Fri 11am–6pm, Sat–Sun 10am–8.30pm, Apr–June daily 10am–8.30pm, July–Aug Mon–Fri 10am–8.30pm, Sat–Sun until 9.30pm, with exceptions). Europe's tallest observation wheel was built to mark the turn of the millennium. At 450ft (135m), it is one of the highest structures in London. The 32 enclosed capsules, each holding 25 people, take 30 minutes to make a full rotation – a speed slow enough to allow passengers to step in and out while the wheel keeps moving. On a clear day, you can see for 25 miles (40km).

THE SOUTHBANK CENTRE

East along the river from the London Eye is the **Southbank Centre** ㉑ (www.southbankcentre.co.uk), Europe's largest arts complex, housing concert halls, a gallery, cinema and theatre. Developments in the 2000s greatly improved the area around the centre, which is now packed with lively restaurants and bars. The **Royal Festival Hall**, the only permanent building designed for the 1951 Festival of Britain, is a major music venue. In 1967 the 2,900-seat hall gained two neighbours: the 917-seater Queen Elizabeth Hall, for chamber concerts, music theatre and opera, and the more intimate, 372-seat Purcell Room. On the upper level of the Southbank Centre complex is the **Hayward Gallery**. The gallery's programme of changing exhibitions focuses on single artists, historical themes and artistic movements, other cultures, and contemporary themes.

Next door is **BFI Southbank** (www.bfi.org.uk), Britain's leading art-house cinema since 1952. With four screens, an interactive 'mediathèque' and a riverfront bar and café, it holds over 2,400 annual screenings and events, from silent movies (some with live piano accompaniment) to world cinema.

The final building in the complex is the **National Theatre** (www.nationaltheatre.org.uk). Opened in 1976, it houses three separate theatres under one roof: the 1,200-seater Olivier, the 900-seater Lyttelton and the intimate Cottesloe with galleries on three sides.

AROUND WATERLOO

A detour from the South Bank along Waterloo Road takes you past the cylindrical **BFI IMAX Cinema** (www.bfi.org.uk/bfi-imax). Where Waterloo Road meets The Cut is the **Old Vic** theatre (www.old-victheatre.com), founded in 1818. Further along The Cut, the **Young Vic** (www.youngvic.org) stages experimental plays giving young directors a chance to develop their art.

Imperial War Museum

South of Waterloo station is the **Imperial War Museum** ㉒ (Lambeth Road; www.iwm.org.uk; daily 10am–6pm; free). Located in the 1811 Bethlehem hospital for the insane, there is much civilian material from both world wars on display, along with a Spitfire and a Harrier Jump Jet in the building's famous atrium. An audio-visual display recreates a wartime air raid on a London street, and visitors can experience conditions in the trenches during World War I. The museum's Holocaust Exhibition is built around the testimonies of survivors, from the origins of anti-Semitism to its horrific conclusion.

AROUND GABRIEL'S WHARF

East of the National Theatre is **Gabriel's Wharf**, a group of shops and restaurants backed by a striking set of *trompe l'œil* paintings. Set back from the river, the Art Deco **Oxo Tower** has pinprick windows outlining the word 'Oxo', a gimmick that the makers of the beef extract of the same name designed to get round a ban on riverfront advertising. The tower has a public viewing gallery and an excellent restaurant.

Further east, just beyond Blackfriars Bridge, which is home to Blackfriars station, the riverside walk leads past the **Bankside Gallery** (www.banksidegallery.com; daily 11am–6pm during exhibitions; free), home of the Royal Watercolour Society and Royal Society of Painter-Printmakers.

TATE MODERN

Easily identifiable by its tall brick chimney, **Tate Modern** ❷❸ (Bankside; www.tate.org.uk; Sun–Thu 10am–6pm, Fri–Sat 10am–10pm; free) occupies the former Bankside Power Station and houses the Tate's international modern collection and part of its contemporary collection. The main entrance, to the west of the building, leads into the ground floor through a broad sweep of glass doors and then down a massive concrete ramp. The impressive space rising six storeys ahead is the Turbine Hall, the old boiler room now used to house massive art installations. A bridge across the Turbine Hall links level four with the Blavatnik Building, also designed by renowned architects Herzog & de Meuron. Its twisted pyramid shape adds a new dimension to London's skyline and there are stunning views from the roof terrace and restaurant.

The permanent collection, including work by Picasso, Matisse, Mondrian, Duchamp, Dalí, Bacon, Pollock, Rothko and Warhol, plus sculpture by Giacometti, Hepworth and Epstein, is displayed in four suites over two floors. On level 2 you will find 'Citizens and States' where the focus is how artists relate to the society in which they live; look out for Picasso's Weeping Woman (1937), which is displayed in the Civil War room 3. Also on level 2 is 'Making Traces' with

Mark Rothko's brooding Seagram murals at its heart. Level 3 presents changing exhibitions, while on level 4 are 'Material Worlds', showcasing artists exploring forms and textures, and 'Media Networks' which looks at the way artists have responded to the constant changes in technology. To beat the crowds, visit on Friday or Saturday evening.

Inside the Tate Modern

THE MILLENNIUM BRIDGE

Providing a link across the Thames from Tate Modern to St Paul's, as well as some spectacular views up and down the river, is Norman Foster's **Millennium Bridge**. Said to resemble a 'blade of light' when floodlit, the cables on this innovative suspension bridge are strung horizontally rather than vertically.

SHAKESPEARE'S GLOBE

Bankside and Southwark are the South Bank's most historic areas. They grew up in competition with the City across the river, but by the 16th century had become dens of vice. Bankside was famous for brothels, bear- and bull-baiting pits, prize fights and the first playhouses, including **Shakespeare's Globe** (21 New Globe Walk; www.shakespearesglobe.com; tours hourly 9.30am–5pm, unless performances running). The replica of the 1599 building opened in 1996 and is worth a visit even if you're

The Globe Theatre

not seeing a play. Thanks to the efforts of the actor Sam Wanamaker, who sadly died before the project was completed, the Globe has been re-created using original construction methods. The open-air galleried theatre accommodates 1,500 people – 600 standing (and liable to get wet if it rains) and 900 seated. The season runs mid-Apr–mid-Oct, but the exquisite indoor Sam Wanamaker Playhouse is open year-round.

Shakespeare's plays were not only shown at the Globe but also at the **Rose Theatre** (www.rosetheatre.org.uk), Bankside's first playhouse, built in 1587, but pulled down in the early 17th century. The foundations were discovered in 1989 and a campaign to restore it began. The Rose reopened in 1999 and today the indoor archaeological site can be visited every Saturday between noon and 4pm.

SOUTHWARK

Back on the riverside walk, by Southwark Bridge, is the **Anchor Inn**. The present building (1770–5) is the sole survivor of the 22 busy inns that once lined Bankside. Just behind a single gable wall remains of **Winchester Palace**, the former 13th-century London residence of the Bishop of Winchester. The powerful bishops had their own laws, regulated local brothels and were the first authority in England to lock up miscreants. The prison they founded, in Clink Street, remained a lock-up until the 18th century, and the word 'clink' became a euphemism for jail. The **Clink Prison Museum** (1 Clink Street; www.clink.co.uk; July–Sept daily 10am–9pm, Oct–June Mon–Fri 10am–6pm, Sat–Sun until 7.30pm) recalls the area's seedy past.

Clink Street leads to Pickfords Wharf, built in 1864 for storing hops, flour and seeds. At the end of the street, in the St Mary Overie Dock, is a full-size replica of Sir Francis Drake's 16th-century galleon, the **Golden Hinde** (Clink Street; www.goldenhinde.com; daily 10am–5pm, Apr–Oct until 6pm). The ship, launched in 1973, is the only replica to have completed a circumnavigation of the globe. It has now clocked up more nautical miles than the original.

Southwark Cathedral and Borough

Southwest of London Bridge and hemmed in by the railway, is **Southwark Cathedral** ❷❹ (http://cathedral.southwark.anglican. org; daily 8am–6pm; free). In the 12th century it was a priory church, and it has a Norman north door, early Gothic work and a number of medieval ornaments. Shakespeare was a parishioner here, and a memorial in the south aisle, paid for by public subscription in 1912, shows him reclining in front of a frieze of 16th-century Bankside; above it is a modern stained-glass window depicting characters from his plays. John Harvard, who gave his name to the American university, was baptised here, and is commemorated in the Harvard Chapel.

Near the cathedral is **Borough Market** (www.boroughmarket. org.uk), which despite its smart glass and steel frontage on Borough High Street, dates back to the 13th century. Now a gourmet market (and an increasingly popular tourist destination), it has over 100 stalls, many offering high-quality takeaway meals. The full market is held on Wednesday and Thursday (10am–5pm), Fridays (10am–6pm) and Saturdays (8am–5pm), with a smaller number of stalls mostly catering to the lunch

Fresh produce at Borough Market

trade open on Monday and Tuesday (10am–5pm); also open on Sunday (noon–4pm) throughout most of December. It isn't cheap, but the quality is high, and you can often try before you buy. Apart from organic basics such as fruit and vegetables, there is a wide choice of more unusual food, with stalls specialising in potted shrimps, game and Spanish ingredients.

Across Borough High Street from the cathedral, the **Old Operating Theatre and Herb Garret** (9a St Thomas Street; www.oldoperatingtheatre.com; Mon 2–5pm, Tue–Sun 10.30am–5pm) is Britain's only surviving 19th-century operating theatre. The Herb Garret, once a store and curing place for herbs, now documents their use in 19th-century medicine.

East along St Thomas Street is the Western Europe's tallest building, **The Shard** ㉕. Designed by Renzo Piano, the behemoth towers 1,016ft (310 metres) over London Bridge station next door and has sparked massive regeneration in the area. If you have a head for heights, you can take a lift up to the 72nd floor (entrance on Joiner Street; www.theviewfromtheshard.com; Apr–Oct daily 10am–10pm, Nov–Mar Sun–Wed 10am–8pm, with exceptions on some Saturdays) for unobstructed views of the city and beyond. Advance booking is recommended, although it is sensible to check the weather first, as mist (particularly in the mornings) often clouds the upper part of the tower.

For excellent food and drink options, continue east for a couple of minutes, to reach Bermondsey Street. This fashionable strip is also home to Zandra Rhodes' colourful Fashion and Textile Museum (83 Bermondsey Street; www.ftmlondon.org; Tue–Sat 11am–6pm, Thu until 8pm, Sun until 5pm), which puts on changing exhibitions exploring fashion, textiles and jewellery. Further along the street, at No. 144–152, is **White Cube** (http://whitecube.com; Tue–Sat 10am–6pm, Sun noon–6pm), the largest of the celebrity gallery owner Jay Jopling's sites.

The Pool of London

Between London Bridge and Tower Bridge is the Upper Pool of London, a former hive of waterborne trade. **Hay's Galleria**, with its shops, stalls and restaurants, marks the first of the Surrey Docks on the south bank. **HMS** *Belfast*, a World War II cruiser, is moored here as a museum (www.iwm.org.uk/visits/hms-belfast; daily 10am–6pm, last admission 1 hour before closing). To its east, the spherical building is **City Hall** (Mon–Thu 8.30am–6pm, Fri until 5.30pm), home to the Mayor of London and the Greater London Authority (the body that governs London).

TOWER BRIDGE

The elaborate Gothic-style bridge looming into sight as you walk east is **Tower Bridge** ㉖. In the 19th century, a time of great industrial expansion, there was a need to improve circulation

HMS Belfast

over the river without hindering the access of ships into London's docks. The result was this triumph of Victorian engineering, built between 1886 and 1894, a bridge that could be raised, made from a steel frame held together with 3 million rivets and clad with decorative stonework. The bridge was opened amid great celebration by the then-Prince and Princess of Wales, on 30 June 1894. The entrance to the **Tower Bridge Exhibition** (www.towerbridge.org.uk; daily Apr–Sept 10am–5.30pm, Oct–Mar 9.30am–5pm) is on the north bank of the Thames. The semi-guided tour takes visitors through the bridge's history, from the controversy that raged over the need to construct it, to its electrification in 1977. You also get the chance to see the engine rooms and walk along a glass floor above its walkways.

BUTLERS WHARF

The old warehouses located just east of Tower Bridge contain a gourmet's delight. The gourmet in question is Habitat founder Sir Terence Conran, who has opened up several restaurants in the biscuit-coloured **Butlers Wharf**. Originally completed in 1873, and once the largest warehouse complex on the Thames, Butlers Wharf closed in 1972. In 1985 a development team chaired by Conran began transforming the area's buildings into a stylish shopping, dining and residential area at a cost of £100 million.

THE CITY

For most of the capital's 2,000-year history, the area between St Paul's and the Tower – generally referred to as the 'Square Mile' – was London. Still known as 'The City', it has its own local government, led by a Lord Mayor, and its own police force. The network of medieval alleys and back streets is still evident, but today's tall buildings hum with banks of computers processing international finance. Teeming with life on weekdays, the City is virtually deserted at weekends.

The Square Mile extends from the highly ornate Law Courts (located at the junction of the Strand and Fleet Street) to the west, to the Tower of London to the east, and from the Barbican in the north to the Thames to the south. This was the area originally enclosed by the Roman Wall, but it is now firmly held in place by commerce.

LEGAL LONDON

Legal London starts at the edge of the City with the **Royal Courts of Justice** (better known as the Law Courts; www.justice.gov.uk), in an elaborate late 19th-century building on the Strand. On the other side of busy Fleet Street, a few steps along, a tiny alleyway leads to the gas-lit sanctuary of the area known as the Temple, which houses two of the four Inns of Court – Inner Temple and Middle Temple (not open to the public). In former times these were the residences of barristers and barristers-in-training, and today's barristers-in-training must still be members of an Inn. The Temple takes its name from its 12th- and 13th-century function as the home of the crusading Knights Templar.

On Chancery Lane is Lincoln's Inn, the oldest of the four Inns of Court. On a large square adjacent is **Sir John Soane's Museum** (13 Lincoln's Inn Fields; www.soane.org; Wed–Sun

The Royal Courts of Justice

10am–5pm, last entry 4.30pm; free except Lates, last Fri of month), the former home of a prominent late 18th-century London architect. The house is just as Soane left it, packed from floor to ceiling with priceless treasures, such as paintings by Hogarth (notably *The Rake's Progress* series), Turner and Canaletto. Off Fleet Street, famous as the former centre of English newspaper production, is **Dr Samuel Johnson's House** (17 Gough Square; www.drjohnsonshouse.org; Mon–Sat 11am–5pm, until 5.30pm May–Sept). It was here that Samuel Johnson lived from 1748 to 1759, compiling his dictionary in the garret with six poor copyists.

ST PAUL'S CATHEDRAL

St Paul's ㉗ (www.stpauls.co.uk; Mon–Sat 8.30am–4pm), the first purpose-built Protestant cathedral, is Sir Christopher Wren's greatest work. A tablet above Wren's plain marble tomb in the crypt reads: *Lector, si monumentum requiris, circumspice* (Reader, if you wish to see his memorial, look around you). Although Westminster Abbey hosts more national occasions, Churchill lay in state here in 1965, and Prince Charles married Diana Spencer here in 1981.

Historians believe that the first church on this site was built in the 7th century, although it came into its own as Old St

Paul's only in the 14th century. By the 16th century St Paul's was the tallest cathedral in England. Much of the building was destroyed in the Great Fire of 1666. Construction on the new St Paul's Cathedral began in 1675, when Wren was 43.

The architect was an old man of 78 when his son Christopher finally laid the highest stone of the lantern on the central cupola in 1710. In total, the cathedral cost £747,954 to build, and most of the money was raised through taxing coal arriving at the port of London. The building is massive and the Portland stone dome alone – exceeded in size only by St Peter's in Rome – weighs over 50,000 tons. Generations have giggled secret messages in St Paul's Whispering Gallery, over 100ft (30m) of perfect acoustics. You have to climb 257 steps to reach it, however, and a further 270 to enjoy the view from the highest of the dome's three galleries.

In the cathedral's crypt, the largest vault of its kind in Europe, is a treasury containing ceremonial vessels, a burial chamber and a chapel dedicated to members of the Order of the British Empire (OBE). The highlights of this cavernous undercroft include the tombs of the Duke of Wellington (whose casket was so huge that it had to be lowered into its resting place via a hole in the Cathedral floor) and of Admiral Lord Nelson, who was foresighted enough to take a coffin with him to the Battle of Trafalgar.

THE BARBICAN

North of the City is the concrete **Barbican** ❷ (Silk Street; www.barbican.org.uk), an arts and conference centre opened in 1982. The cultural offerings here include art galleries, theatres, a concert hall (the Barbican is the home of the London Symphony Orchestra), cinema, a library, bars and restaurants.

Just outside the arts centre is the **Museum of London** (150 London Wall; www.museumoflondon.org.uk; daily 10am–6pm;

Spectacular St Paul's Cathedral

free), which charts every aspect of the capital's long history.

THE FINANCIAL CITY

The heart of the business district of the City focuses on the **Bank of England** ㉙ (nicknamed 'The Old Lady of Threadneedle Street'). Imposing windowless walls rise impregnably, with seven stories above ground and three below. This is where the nation's gold reserves are kept.

Opposite the Bank of England is the neoclassical **Mansion House**, residence of the Lord Mayor of London. Adjacent is Wren's **St Stephen Walbrook**, whose dome is said to have been a rehearsal for St Paul's.

Northwest of the Bank is the **Guildhall** (Basinghall Street; www.guildhall.cityoflondon.gov.uk; opening times vary subject to events taking place at the Guildhall; free), the town hall of the City of London. This building dates from 1411 and withstood the Great Fire and the Blitz. Step inside when open to the public to see the ancient Great Hall. Here the centuries-old functions and ceremonies continue: banquets of state, the annual swearing-in of the new Lord Mayor in November and meetings of the Court of Common Council. The adjacent Art Gallery (Mon–Sat 10am–5pm, Sun noon–4pm; free) is well worth a visit too – the remains of a Roman amphitheatre are visible on the lower floor.

East of the Bank of England, along the ancient thoroughfares of Cornhill and Leadenhall Street, is **Lloyd's of London**. Lloyd's originated in 1688 in Edward Lloyd's Coffee House, where ships' captains, owners and merchants gathered to do marine insurance deals. Lloyd's moved to Richard Rogers' space-age building in 1986. A huge atrium rises 200ft (60m) at the heart of this steel-and-glass structure which, like Rogers' Pompidou Centre, exposes its workings to view.

In the shadow of Lloyd's is the Victorian **Leadenhall Market**, once the wholesale market for poultry and game, and now a handsome commercial centre. It has been prettified, and its magnificent Victorian cream-and-maroon structure now houses sandwich bars, restaurants and upmarket fashion chain stores, which attract city workers at breakfast and lunchtime.

South of Leadenhall Market, back towards the river, is Christopher Wren's 202ft (62 metre) high **Monument** (Monument Yard; www.themonument.info; daily 9.30am–6pm, until 5.30pm in winter), topped with a gleaming gold urn of fire. The Roman Doric column was designed to commemorate the victims of the Great Fire, which destroyed 13,200 houses and 87 churches. Its height matches the distance from the spot in Pudding Lane, where the fire is believed to have started. There are 311 stairs up to the encaged viewing platform at the top.

THE TOWER OF LONDON

East of the Monument, on the north bank of the Thames is the **Tower of London** ❸⓿ (Tower Hill; www.hrp.org.uk; Tue–Sat 9am–5.30pm, Sun–Mon 10am–5.30pm, until 4.30pm in winter). Encircled by a moat (now dry) and with 22 towers, the building was begun by William the Conqueror in 1078. Over the years its buildings have served as a fort, arsenal, palace and prison, and housed a treasury, public record office, observatory, royal mint and zoo.

At the centre of the complex is the White Tower, designed by the Norman monk Gandulf for William the Conqueror. The Tower's walls are 15ft (5m) thick and contain the fine Norman Chapel of St John on the first floor. Henry VIII added the domestic architecture of the Queen's House behind the Tower on the left, which is where the Tower's governor lives. The 19th-century Museum and Waterloo Barracks, to the right of the Tower, contain the Jewel House where the **Crown Jewels** are a major attraction. At the centre of the display are a dozen crowns and a glittering array of swords, sceptres and orbs.

The Gherkin

The Imperial State Crown, made in 1937, has 2,868 diamonds and is topped with an 11th-century sapphire. A moving walkway speeds you past the treasures, so, rather disappointingly, you can't linger.

Look out for the Tower ravens; according to legend, if they ever leave, the Tower and England will fall. Ravens are bred and their wings are clipped to ensure they stay. Also look out for the Beefeaters, who guard the tower and act as guides.

KENSINGTON AND CHELSEA

The Royal Borough of Kensington and Chelsea is central London's most expensive residential area. It is home to upmarket shops such as Harrods and Harvey Nichols, designer row Sloane Street, and also takes in the King's Road, an influential fashion stretch in the 1960s. The borough has a royal palace, a fine park and a clutch of world-renowned museums.

The Gherkin

Although 30 St Mary Axe is one of the City's most iconic sights, that name alone means little to most. More familiar is its nickname, 'The Gherkin', inspired by the tower's distinctive shape. The City has seen more towers on the skyline with nicknames due to distinctive shapes including the Leadenhall Building known as the 'Cheesegrater' and the 'Walkie Talkie' aka 20 Fenchurch Street.

HYDE PARK AND KENSINGTON GARDENS

Hyde Park and the adjoining Kensington Gardens cover one square mile (2.5 sq km) – the same area as the City of London. Although they are a single open space, they are two distinct parks, divided by the Ring or West Carriage Drive.

Hyde Park Corner, at the western end of Piccadilly, is a good place to enter the park. Near the entrance to the park, facing **Wellington Arch**, is Apsley House, which has the enviable address of No. 1, London. Built by Robert Adam for the Duke of Wellington, it is now home to the **Apsley House Art Collection** (www.english-heritage.org.uk/daysout/properties/apsley-house; Apr–Oct Wed–Sun 11am–5pm, Nov–Mar Sat–Sun 10am–4pm) and has a fine collection of Old Master paintings and memorabilia linked with the Duke. Highlights include Canova's larger-than-life nude statue of Napoleon, one of numerous items in his house depicting the Duke's great foe, and a magnificent reconstruction of the Waterloo Banquet.

The Domesday Book of 1086 records that wild bulls and boars once inhabited **Hyde Park** ㉛. The park was first owned by the monks of Westminster Abbey, but after ecclesiastic property was confiscated during the Dissolution of the Monasteries, Henry VIII turned it into a royal hunting ground. The park was opened to the public in the 17th century and then sold off in chunks by Oliver Cromwell, the Lord Protector.

At the northeast corner of the park is the monumental **Marble Arch**, erected in 1827 in front of Buckingham Palace and moved here in 1851 when it proved too narrow for the State coaches to pass through. The traffic island in which it now resides was the site of Tyburn Tree, a triangular gallows on which an estimated 50,000 people were publicly hanged between 1571 and 1759. Just inside the park is **Speaker's Corner**, where anyone can pull up a soap box and sound off – a tradition going back to the days when condemned men were allowed to have a last word.

The lake at the centre of both parks is called the **Serpentine** in Hyde Park and the **Long Water** in Kensington Gardens. It was created in the 1730s as a boating pond, and boats can still be hired from the north bank. On the Kensington Gardens side, next to the lake, is a statue of J.M. Barrie's **Peter Pan**. According to tradition, at 9am every Christmas Day, hardy swimmers dive into the lake to compete for the Peter Pan Cup. On the south side of the Serpentine is the **Diana, Princess of Wales Memorial Fountain**, a circular ring of flowing water that you can dip your feet in. The **Serpentine Gallery** (www.serpentinegallery.org; Tue–Sun 10am–6pm; free), housed in a 1930s teahouse, stages cutting-edge art shows. Past subjects include

Man Ray, Henry Moore and Cindy Sherman. A short walk from the gallery is the Serpentine Sackler Gallery (times as main gallery) designed by architect Zaha Hadid and incorporating The Magazine, a listed neoclassical gunpowder store dating from 1805.

Boating on the Serpentine, Hyde Park

South of the gallery is the **Albert Memorial**, a gilded tribute to Queen Victoria's consort. Designed by Sir George Gilbert Scott, it depicts the Prince as a god or philosopher, holding the catalogue of the Great Exhibition. Opposite, just outside the park, is another of Victoria's tokens to her husband, the **Royal Albert Hall** (Kensington Gore; www.royalalberthall.com; charge for tours). There are various themed tours of the ornate concert hall, such as the Victorian tours, behind-the-scenes tours and a tour that includes afternoon tea.

Kensington Gardens were once the private gardens of **Kensington Palace** (www.hrp.org.uk; palace Mar–Oct 10am–6pm, Nov–Feb 10am–4pm; last admission 1 hour before closing). The palace has been a royal household ever since the asthmatic William of Orange fled damp, polluted Whitehall. A number of monarchs were born here, most recently Victoria in 1819. A number of members of the royal household live in the private side of the palace, with the newest inhabitants being the Duke and Duchess of Cambridge and their three children, Prince George, Princess Charlotte and Prince Louis.

To the north of the gardens is the **Diana, Princess of Wales Memorial Playground** (www.royalparks.org.uk; daily from 10am, May–Aug until 7.45pm, Apr and Sept until 6.45pm, Mar and early Oct until 5.45pm, Feb and late Oct until 4.45pm, Nov–Jan until 3.45pm), commemorating the late Princess, who lived at Kensington Palace at the time of her death. A huge wooden Peter Pan-inspired pirate ship on a sandy 'beach', wigwams and sensory trails offer hours of fun for children.

KENSINGTON

A few yards from the peace of these parks is busy **Kensington High Street**, which is dominated by chain stores. However, if you take a few steps off this main thoroughfare you will find elegant squares with gorgeous old houses. Situated just next to the neo-Gothic church of St Mary Abbots is **Kensington Church Street**, famed for its antiques shops. At the west end of Kensington High Street is the wooded **Holland Park**, home to a blitzed Jacobean mansion, Holland House, with Japanese gardens and peacocks.

At 12 Holland Park Road is **Leighton House** (Wed–Mon 10am–5.30pm), the home of the Victorian artist Lord Frederic Leighton from 1866 until he died in 1896. The *pièce de résistance* is the Arab Hall, inspired by a Moorish palace in Palermo. Almost next door is the Commonwealth Institute, home to the **Design Museum** (www.designmuseum.org; daily 10am–6pm, first Fri of month until 8pm), which presents exhibitions related to architectural, industrial, fashion, graphic and product design.

SOUTH KENSINGTON

Familiarly known as 'South Ken', this area is best known for its museums, a legacy of the Great Exhibition of 1851, at which Prince Albert raised money to purchase 87 acres (35 hectares) of land in South Kensington and make this the 'muse-umland' of London. South Kensington has a large French population, which makes for a number of very good patisseries and some of the best French bookshops in London.

The Royal Albert Hall

Natural History Museum

On Cromwell Road is the impressive neo-Gothic pile of the **Natural History Museum** ㉜ (www.nhm.ac.uk; daily 10am–5.50pm; free except for some special exhibitions), built from 1873–80. The museum's biggest draw is undoubtedly the Dinosaur Gallery – there is also a crowd-pleasing animated model of a Tyrannosaurus Rex, which roars and smells authentically unpleasant. Other highlights include a life-size model of a blue whale, a simulated earthquake in a mock-up of a Japanese super-market and an escalator that rises up through a rotating model of the globe, giving the sensation that you, and not the globe, are turning.

The Darwin Centre's Cocoon building is a futuristic home for the museum's enormous insect and plant collection. The cathedral-like Hintze Hall is home to Hope, a huge blue whale skeleton suspended from the ceiling, which took the place of previous resident Dippy, a bronze diplodocus skeleton cast that was on display for over three decades.

The Natural History Museum

Science Museum

Next door is the **Science Museum** (www.sciencemuseum.org.uk; daily 10am–6pm; free), which traces the history of inventions from the first steam train to the battered command module from the *Apollo 10* space mission. Seven floors of exhibition space cover computing, medicine, photography, chemistry and physics. There are imaginative exhibits on genes and the future of digital communications. The Flight Zone houses an IMAX cinema and some flight simulators, while a maths and science interactive gallery offers a giant walk-through model of the solar system and the opportunity to take part in chemistry experiments.

Victoria and Albert Museum

The first director of the **Victoria and Albert Museum** (V&A; Cromwell Road; www.vam.ac.uk; daily 10am–5.45pm, Fri until 10pm; free except for special exhibitions), Henry Cole, began assembling the museum's collection the year after the 1851 Great Exhibition. However, Queen Victoria only laid the foundation stone of the current building in 1899, 38 years after Albert died. Its 1909 façade is by Aston Webb, who also designed the front of Buckingham Palace. Inside is the richest collection of decorative arts in the world, exhibited in beautiful galleries that have been cleverly remodelled to showcase the latest in modern design.

The collection includes extraordinary groupings of sculpture, pottery, china, engravings, illustrations, metalwork, paintings, textiles, period costumes and furniture. Upstairs, on level 3, the V&A's Photography Centre, which opened in 2018, displays artworks and artefacts tracing photography from its invention to the present day.

On the far side of the John Madejski Garden are the spectacular Arts and Crafts-designed Morris, Gamble and Poynter rooms, with their stained glass and Minton tiles. Originally designed as the museum's refreshment rooms, they have been restored to their intended function as a delightful café. Sitting alongside the Henry Cole Wing on Exhibition Road, the grand porticoed Blavatnik Hall, designed by London-based architect Amanda Levete, was added in 2017. It includes the subterranean

◎ PORTOBELLO ROAD MARKET

Notting Hill is a gentrified residential area with some of the grandest Georgian townhouses in the capital. The area is also home to the annual Notting Hill Carnival and the Portobello Road Market. Built on the site of a pig farm named after an English victory over Spain at Porto Bello in the Gulf of Mexico in 1739, it has developed over the past 50 years into a major antiques market.

The road accommodates three markets (Mon–Wed 9am–6pm, Fri–Sat 9am–7pm, Thu 9am–1pm, with exceptions). The antiques market, at the south end, merges into a food market where the traditional fruit-and-vegetable stalls sit alongside more exotic foodstuffs from around the world. A flea market mixing genuine junk with cutting-edge fashion operates under the Westway flyover, at the north end.

Sainsbury Gallery for temporary exhibitions and a porcelain-tiled courtyard and café.

KNIGHTSBRIDGE

Just south of Hyde Park, Knightsbridge is one of the most expensive chunks of real estate in London and home to **Harrods ㉝**, one of the world's most famous department stores. Opened by Henry Charles Harrod in 1849 as a small grocer's shop, the present terracotta palace – whose façade is lit by some 11,500 light bulbs at night – was built at the turn of the 20th century. Until 2010, the shop was owned by Mohamed Al Fayed, an Egyptian businessman whose son Dodi died with Princess Diana in the Paris car crash. Staff claim to be able to source any item you want, and the shop even has a dress code,

Tipu's Tiger at the V&A

which security men on the door ensure is enforced. The vast Edwardian Food Halls are a major attraction, exquisitely decorated with around 1,900 Art Nouveau tiles.

Southwest of Harrods and its more fashionable neighbour, **Harvey Nichols**, is Beauchamp (pronounced 'Beecham') Place. The former village high street is now home to some pricey restaurants and designer shops. **Sloane Street**, a major shopping artery, has back-to-back designer labels and connects Knightsbridge with Chelsea.

CHELSEA

Chelsea has long been at the cutting edge of London fashion. Mary Quant started it with the first boutique (long-gone) on the King's Road, and from the World's End (430 King's Road) avant-garde designer Vivienne Westwood and Malcolm McLaren gave the world punk in the late 1970s. Chelsea in the 21st century is more subdued, and the **King's Road** tends nowadays towards chain stores; however, a walk along it is still good for people-watching.

Where Sloane Street meets the King's Road is **Sloane Square ㉞**, named after Sir Hans Sloane, whose collection formed the basis of the British Museum. Close to the square, the Duke of York's HQ now houses the **Saatchi Gallery** (www.saatchigallery. com; daily 10am–6pm, last admission at 5.30pm; free). The gallery showcases the work of contemporary artists assembled by former advertising mogul Charles Saatchi, who was an early purchaser of work by one-time YBAs (Young British Artists) such as Tracey Emin's *My Bed* and Damien Hirst's shark in formaldehyde. In 2010 Saatchi announced that he would be gifting the gallery to the nation – today, it hosts an ever-changing roster of art installations and displays by emerging artists

The **Royal Hospital** on Chelsea Bridge Road, has been a Chelsea landmark since 1692. It is home to the Chelsea Pensioners, known for their scarlet coats, a design that dates back to the 18th century. Between here and the Embankment are Ranelagh Gardens, which host the RHS Chelsea Flower Show (www.rhs.org.uk) every spring. Next to the hospital is the **National Army Museum** (www. nam.ac.uk; daily 10am–5.30pm, last admission at 5pm). Continue down to the River Thames along Royal Hospital Road and turn into

Leafy Cheyne Walk in Chelsea

Tite Street. This attractive residential area is the epitome of bourgeois respectability but in the early 19th century it was very bohemian. Look out for the blue plaques on the street dedicated to Oscar Wilde (No 34) and John Singer Sargent (No 31). Turn right on to the Embankment. For garden lovers, take a right down Swan Walk for the **Chelsea Physic Garden** (www.chelseaphysicgarden. co.uk; Apr–Oct Mon–Fri, Sun 11am–6pm, Feb–Mar Mon–Fri 10am–4pm), second only to the one in Oxford as the oldest botanic garden in the country. Back on the Embankment ahead is **Cheyne Walk**. The splendid houses here were on the water's edge until the reclamation of the Embankment in the 19th century. Blue plaques mark the former homes of pre-Raphaelite painter Dante Gabriel Rosetti as well as the author George Eliot. Just off Cheyne Walk is **Carlyle's House** (24 Cheyne Row; www.nationaltrust.org.uk/carlyles-house; Mar–Oct Wed–Sun 11am–5pm), home of the Victorian writer, Thomas Carlyle, until his death in 1881.

NORTH LONDON

Easily accessible by Underground, North London has many attractions, including upmarket Hampstead, notable for its heath and literary connections, neighbouring Highgate with its cemetery, and elegant Islington, the stomping ground of the chattering classes. Camden is worth a visit for its busy, bohemian market and its pleasant canal area.

ISLINGTON

This borough, widely regarded as the territory of well-heeled socialists, symbolises the gentrification of London's Georgian and Victorian dwellings. Classic terraces can be found in areas such as Canonbury Square, where authors George Orwell and Evelyn Waugh once lived. The square is home to the **Estorick Collection** (39a Canonbury Square; www.estorickcollection. com; Wed–Sat 11am–6pm, Sun noon–5pm), a showcase for modern Italian art.

The crossroads at the heart of Islington's shopping district is called the Angel, named after a long-gone coaching inn. Adjacent is **Camden Passage**, an upmarket antiques arcade; more affordable bargains can be had at the street market held here on Wednesday and Saturday (9am–6pm), with some stalls also on Friday (10am–6pm) and Sunday (11am–6pm). At the south end of Islington is **Sadler's Wells** (Rosebery Avenue; www.sadlerswells.com), London's top modern dance venue. Now housed in a modern, glass-fronted building, the original theatre dates back to 1683.

CAMDEN

Markets are the main attraction in **Camden ③**. Cheap clothes aimed at the young are sold at Camden High Street (daily 10am–6pm), while crafts are on offer at **Camden Lock Market**, off Chalk Farm Road (daily 10am–6pm; www.camdenlock.net). Camden Lock is on the Regent's Canal, an 8.5-mile (14km) stretch of water running from Paddington to Limehouse in Docklands.

Shopping at Camden Passage

HAMPSTEAD AND HIGHGATE

Exclusive **Hampstead** ⠀③⑥ has long been a desirable address, especially among the successful literary set, and it still has its fair share of wealthy celebrity residents. Open spaces predominate. The 3-sq-mile (8-sq-km) **Heath** is the main 'green lung', with Parliament Hill on its south side giving splendid views across London, as does the 112-acre (45-hectare) **Primrose Hill** overlooking Regent's Park to the south. These are all welcome areas of parkland over which locals stride, walk dogs, fly kites, skate and swim in the segregated ponds.

The elegant **Kenwood House** (Hampstead Lane; www.english-heritage.org.uk/daysout/properties/kenwood; daily Nov–Mar 10am–4pm, Apr–Oct until 5pm; free), which overlooks Hampstead Heath, displays the Iveagh Bequest. The collection includes works by Rembrandt, Reynolds, Turner and Gainsborough.

Sigmund Freud, fleeing the Nazis in 1938, moved from Vienna to Hampstead. The **Freud Museum** (20 Maresfield Gardens; www.freud.org.uk; Wed–Sun noon–5pm) preserves his house as he left it.

A pretty hilltop suburb, **Highgate** is home to the grandest burial ground in London, **Highgate Cemetery** (Swain's Lane; www.highgatecemetery.org; East Cemetery daily 10am–5pm, until 4pm Nov–Feb; West Cemetery by tour only). There are 170,000 people interred here, including Christina Rossetti, George Eliot and Karl Marx (whose tomb was vandalised in February 2019), buried in 53,000 graves.

EAST LONDON

This part of London was the first stop for many successive waves of immigrants, whose labour helped to fuel the Industrial Revolution and build the docks through which much of the British Empire's trade passed. Poverty and overcrowding were endemic. Although many areas remain poor, a growing number have now been gentrified and are considered to be quite trendy. Further east still, in Stratford, there has been extensive regeneration – including the construction of Europe's largest shopping centre, Westfield Stratford City – kick-started by the preparations for the London 2012 Olympics.

SPITALFIELDS AND WHITECHAPEL

Just east of Liverpool Street is **Old Spitalfields Market** ㊲ (www.oldspitalfieldsmarket.com), a former fruit-and-vegetable market, which has a buzzy bohemian craft, clothing and organic food market (daily) and a modern shopping arcade with fashion and home stores adjacent.

Nearby is a museum with a difference, the wonderfully atmospheric **Dennis Severs' House** (18 Folgate Street; tel: 020 7247 4013; www.dennissevershouse.co.uk; see website for details; booking necessary; curator-led tours selected Saturdays). An American artist, Severs renovated this former 18th-century silk-weaver's house in the 1970s, creating a time capsule that assaults the senses – it looks, smells and sounds as if 18th-century Huguenots still live there.

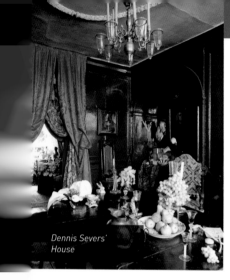

Dennis Severs' House

Southeast of Spitalfields is **Brick Lane**, known for its proliferation of Indian restaurants. On the northern stretch of Brick Lane there are fashionable boutiques and trendy bars, many within the Old Truman Brewery, the self-styled creative hub of the East End.

Responding to the East End's spiritual and economic poverty, a local vicar and his wife founded the **Whitechapel Art Gallery** (Whitechapel High Street; www.whitechapelgallery.org; Tue–Sun 11am–6pm, Thu–Fri until 9pm; free) in 1897. The gallery mounts high-profile shows of cutting-edge art in a lovely airy space; past exhibitions have included Picasso, Mark Rothko and Frida Kahlo.

HOXTON

One of the areas in this eastern part of London to experience a huge degree of gentrification is **Hoxton**, near Old Street. The transformation began when artists moved in, many creating studios in redundant warehouses. Art dealers and designers followed, and urban desolation became urban chic. Commercial galleries radiate from **Hoxton Square**. Café-bars and clothes shops line the streets around Curtain Road, and the area is one of London's most popular places for a night out. On Sundays, Hoxton's **Columbia Road Market** (8am–3pm) specialises in flowers, plants and garden accessories.

DOCKLANDS

In the 1990s, London's docks were transformed. Made derelict by heavy World War II bombing and rendered obsolete by the new container ports to the east, their proximity to the financial institutions of the City made them an attractive location for high-tech office buildings. The 850ft (260m) **Canary Wharf** ㊳ complex, officially called One Canada Square, was the first of several skyscrapers to spring up here. The area is now a lively but somewhat sterile patchwork of glass, steel and concrete, with a large shopping centre underground.

The **Museum of London Docklands** (West India Quay; www.museumoflondon.org.uk/docklands; daily 10am–6pm; free) recounts 2,000 years of local history. Highlights include a 20ft (6 metre) model of Old London Bridge and an evocative exhibition about London's role in the slave trade. There is a lovely play space for young children – Mudlarks (see website for opening times).

STRATFORD

One of the strengths of the London 2012 Olympic Games bid was the promise of large-scale redevelopment of some of the capital's most deprived areas, mainly in the east of the city. Once the events were over, the process began of turning the centrepiece of the Games, the Olympic Park in Stratford, into the **Queen Elizabeth Olympic Park** ㊴ (www.queenelizabetholympicpark.co.uk). The £292m project involved dismantling the temporary venues – such as the hockey and basketball arenas – and turning the site into an area of parkland, with walking and cycling routes and recreational facilities.

Other major venues – the Olympic Stadium, the velodrome and swimming pool – continue to be used for sport. Also open to the public is the 676ft (114.5m) -tall ArcelorMittal Orbit

Skyscrapers in Docklands

(daily 10am–6pm), the giant twisted sculpture designed by Anish Kapoor and Cecil Balmond, housing the world's longest tunnel slide.

SOUTHEAST LONDON

The expansion of the Overground and Jubilee lines into southeast London has opened up this area to those who previously dismissed it for being off the main Tube network. There are many riches here, from historic naval Greenwich to artistic Dulwich.

GREENWICH

Long the favoured destination of nautical and science buffs, **Greenwich** ㊵ enjoyed notoriety in 2000 as the site of the Millennium Dome. The great white tent was built to house a one-year exhibition for the millennium, but was a financial and critical failure. The structure was later relaunched as the **O2 Arena** (www.theo2.co.uk) and is a popular venue for concerts and sporting events (nearest Tube: North Greenwich).

There are plenty of other reasons to visit villagey Greenwich. The district can be covered in half a day and is at its busiest at weekends, when its craft markets are in full swing. One of the nicest ways to arrive is by boat from Westminster or Tower Bridge, although you can also travel by Docklands Light

Railway (DLR) from Bank to Cutty Sark station or by train from London Bridge.

In dry dock on the waterfront is the *Cutty Sark* (King William Walk; www.rmg.co.uk/cuttysark; daily 10am–5pm), a sailing ship from the great days of the tea-clippers that used to race to be the first to bring the new season's tea from China. The ship reopened to the public in 2012 after it was damaged by a serious fire in 2007. Luckily, at the time of the blaze many of the ship's timbers and its striking figurehead had already been removed to allow restoration work to take place. The ship is set in a huge glass chamber, meaning that you can walk underneath it, touch its hull and even sit underneath it at the Even Keel Café.

Much of the land in the area is taken up by lovely **Greenwich Park** (www.royalparks.org.uk/parks/greenwich-park), at the top of which is Sir Christopher Wren's **Royal Observatory** (Greenwich Park; www.rmg.co.uk/royal-observatory; daily 10am–5pm), where Greenwich Mean Time was established in 1884. It is a steep climb to the Observatory, but the views across to Canary Wharf are

Cable car

An addition to London's public transport network, which coincided with the 2012 Olympic Games, is the Emirates Air Line. The cable car that runs between North Greenwich (near the O2) over the Thames to the Royal Docks is a great way to get fabulous views of east London, including the Olympic park and the sweep of the Thames as it heads out to sea. However, it has proved to be an impractical solution for commuters and the number of passenger journeys has declined since the Olympics. You can use your Oyster for a discounted price or buy a ticket online, or at the terminal. For more information, check www.emiratesairline.co.uk.

Dulwich Picture Gallery

splendid. A brass rule on the ground marks the line between the Eastern and Western hemispheres, making it possible to have a foot in both. Nearby is the South Building, housing the **Planetarium**. At the base of the park is the imposing **National Maritime Museum** (Romney Road; www.rmg.co.uk/national-maritime-museum; daily 10am–5pm; free except for special exhibitions), which traces the history both of the Royal Navy and the Merchant Navy, as well as the colonisers and discoverers. An extension houses four immersive galleries, the AHOY! Childrens Gallery and a pleasant café.

Opposite is the **Old Royal Naval College** (King William Walk; www.ornc.org; daily grounds 8am–11pm, hall and chapel 10am–5pm), designed by Wren, Hawksmoor and Vanbrugh, with gardens by André Le Nôtre. It was built as a hospital for naval pensioners to match Wren's Royal Hospital in Chelsea and was designed in two halves to leave the view free to the river from Inigo Jones' small, but perfectly formed **Queen's House** (Romney Road; www.rmg.co.uk/queens-house; daily 10am–5pm; free), a gift to Anne of Denmark from her husband, James. In 2019, the college unveiled its freshly restored Baroque Painted Hall and the new Sackler Gallery. The heart of Greenwich lies to the west of the park, where an attractive, old-fashioned **covered market** and neighbouring Greenwich Church Street are lively at weekends.

DULWICH

With its leafy streets, elegant houses and a spacious park, **Dulwich** ❹ is an oasis of calm. It is largely the creation of one man, Edward Alleyn, an actor-manager who bought land in the area in 1605 and founded an estate to administer a chapel, alms houses and a school for the poor.

The **Dulwich Picture Gallery** (Gallery Road; www.dulwichpicturegallery.org.uk; Tue–Sun 10am–5pm, last admission at 4.30pm) was formed by combining Alleyn's art collection with a bequest of paintings originally intended for a Polish National Gallery, but diverted when the King of Poland was forced to abdicate. The grand building was designed by Sir John Soane and opened in 1814 as the country's first major public art gallery, with works by masters including Rembrandt, Rubens, Gainsborough and Murillo.

SOUTHWEST LONDON

This wealthy area incorporates Wimbledon, synonymous with tennis; genteel Richmond, home to a pleasant shopping centre and a vast area of parkland; Kew, site of the Unesco-protected Kew Gardens; and Hampton Court, where the 16th-century riverside palace was the favourite residence of Henry VIII.

WIMBLEDON, RICHMOND AND KEW

The suburb of Wimbledon hosts Britain's top tennis

The Horniman

Just east of Dulwich, in Forest Hill, is the **Horniman Museum** (100 London Road; www.horniman.ac.uk; daily 10am–5.30pm; free). Founded in 1901 by Frederick Horniman, a tea merchant, the museum houses rich collections of ethnography and natural history.

tournament in June/July (see page 98), and its history is captured in the **Lawn Tennis Museum** (Church Road, Wimbledon; www.wimbledon.com; daily 10am–5pm, last admission at 4.30pm; tours available at additional charge). The area is also known for **Wimbledon Common**, a large partly wooded expanse with nature trails.

The main attraction in Richmond is **Richmond Park** (www.royalparks.org.uk/parks/richmond-park), grazed by herds of red and fallow deer and, at 2,350 acres (950 hectares), the largest of the eight royal parks. The original royal residence in the park is the Palladian White Lodge (1727), now used by the Royal Ballet School. **Richmond Green** is the handsome town centre, lined with some fine 17th- and 18th-century buildings, and the remains of the 12th-century royal palace.

The nearby suburb of **Kew** ㊷ is synonymous with the **Royal Botanic Gardens** (www.kew.org; daily 10am–5.30pm, with exceptions; glasshouses and galleries close half an hour earlier than gardens). The 300-acre (120-hectare) gardens were established in 1759 with the help of Joseph Banks, the botanist who named Botany Bay on Captain James Cook's first voyage to Australia. Other explorers and amateur enthusiasts added their specimens over the centuries, making this a formidable repository and research centre.

The gardens are beautiful, with grand glasshouses including the Palm House, Waterlily House, Princess of Wales Conservatory and Alpine House, and there is an orangery, mock Chinese pagoda, a treetop walkway and the 17th-century Dutch

Ham House

Reached along the towpath at Richmond is Ham House (www.nationaltrust.org.uk/ham-house; Mar–early Oct daily noon–4pm), a furnished 1610 Palladian building set in lovely gardens.

House, a former royal palace where George III was locked up when it was thought that he had gone mad. His wife Charlotte had a summerhouse built in the grounds as a picnic spot.

More recent additions include The Hive, a multisensory installation showing the role of bees in the food chain and the dangers to their population, and a Children's Garden featuring a 4m (13ft) -high canopy walk.

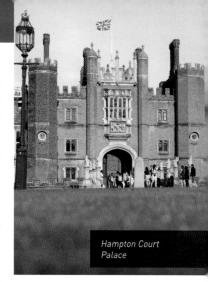
Hampton Court Palace

HAMPTON COURT

Located 14 miles (23km) west of central London and easily accessible by train from Waterloo or by riverboat from Westminster or Richmond, the Tudor **Hampton Court Palace** ㊸ (www.hrp.org. uk/hampton-court-palace; daily 10am–4.30pm, Apr–Oct until 6pm, last admission 1 hour before closing) was built in 1514 for Cardinal Wolsey but appropriated by Henry VIII in 1525, following Wolsey's fall from grace. Surrounded by 60 acres (24 hectares) of immaculate riverside gardens, it was Henry's favourite palace – he spent five of his six honeymoons here. Although the State Apartments are sumptuous, featuring works by such gifted craftsmen as Antonio Verrio and William Kent, the highlights of the visit are the Great Hall and Chapel Royal. Also popular is the 300-year-old palace maze.

Shop in style at Liberty

WHAT TO DO

London has some of the greatest theatres in the world and is at the cutting edge of fashion, music and the arts. For up-to-the-minute entertainment listings consult the weekly events magazine *Time Out* (www.timeout.com/london) or the newspapers *Metro* (www.metro.co.uk) and *The Evening Standard* (www.standard.co.uk), all three free and available at Tube and train stations as well as online. The weekend newspapers usually also include a listings guide – *The Guide*, which comes with Saturday's *Guardian*, is pretty comprehensive.

SHOPPING

With more than 30,000 shops, London is a consumerist heaven, and it is no surprise that people flock here from all over the world just to spend, spend, spend. However specialised your retail needs, you can be sure that somewhere in this sprawling city there is a shop that can meet them. Unlike many other European capitals, Sundays and summer holidays are not sacred; London is a year-round shopping destination.

SHOPPING STREETS AND DISTRICTS

While the size of the city makes it impossible to cover it in a week, from a shopper's point of view London is relatively easy to navigate. The city is loosely divided into shopping districts, each offering its own experience. The underground is usually the quickest means of getting from area to area, while the bus system is excellent but less easy to navigate. Distances between some streets, such as Oxford Street, Tottenham Court Road, Regent Street and Bond Street, are short enough to walk.

Oxford Street is the capital's main shopping thoroughfare, packed from end to end with hundreds of stores. West of Oxford Circus are a collection of large department stores, including upmarket Selfridges, John Lewis, House of Fraser, Debenhams and Marks & Spencer. All the main high-street chains have shops here, including enormous flagship branches of Topshop and Nike (near Oxford Circus) and Primark (near Marble Arch).

The shops on **Regent Street** range from upmarket high-street chains such as All Saints, Anthropologie, COS, Reiss and Superdry to designer brands including Burberry and Karen Millen. It is home to Hamleys (Britain's largest toy shop), the Apple Store, London institution Liberty and, on Lower Regent Street, sports emporium Lillywhites.

Tottenham Court Road is dominated by electronics and home stores. **Charing Cross Road**, while no longer the preserve of second-hand and antiquarian bookshops it once was, is still home to the bookworm's favourite Foyles.

Covent Garden is one of London's most popular retail areas, with shops ranging from high-street and cutting-edge fashion boutiques to quirky specialists selling everything from teapots to kites. Although **Soho** has never quite lost its seedy image, between the sex shops are fine delicatessens as well as some great fashion boutiques selling hip urbanwear.

In the Piccadilly area (the southern end of Regent Street), you'll find the upmarket grocer's **Fortnum & Mason**, notable for its gorgeous window displays, as well as some of London's oldest shops, many of which hold royal warrants to supply the Queen and her family with goods. Nearby **Jermyn Street** specialises in menswear. **Old Bond Street** and **New Bond Street**, in Mayfair, offer a vast choice of designer labels. Savile Row, again in Mayfair, specialises in bespoke tailoring, and Cork Street, with its numerous galleries, is an art-lover's dream.

Even in the mainstream West End there are unusual enclaves lined with boutiques and galleries, such as **St Christopher's Place**. On villagey **Marylebone High Street**, gourmet food shops jostle with upmarket boutiques and several stylish homeware stores, including the branch of the Conran Shop that sparked regeneration along this strip.

The Art Nouveau food hall at Harrods

The City has its very own shopping centre, One New Change, which offers stunning views of St Paul's Cathedral from its 6th floor terrace.

For those wanting the best of European and international designer fashions, **Knightsbridge**, home to the high-class department stores Harrods and Harvey Nichols, has the highest concentration of such shops. Haute couture names from Armani to Yves Saint Laurent sit next to established British designers.

Although the **King's Road** is no longer as trendy as in its sixties heyday, shoppers still flock to it for its concentration of upmarket chain stores, small boutiques and the Peter Jones department store on Sloane Square. **Kensington Church Street** is a favourite destination for antiques lovers. **Notting Hill**, home of Portobello market, also has many fashionable boutiques.

Further west, **Shepherd's Bush** has become one of London's premier shopping destinations since the opening of **Westfield London**. Alongside its high-street stores are numerous restaurants and The Village, a mall-within-a-mall housing premium

A stylish boutique in Mayfair's trendy Dover Street Market

brands including Louis Vuitton and Gucci. Far to the east, by the Queen Elizabeth Olympic Park, is the vast Westfield Stratford City.

MARKETS

London has markets to suit all tastes. Daily, historic covered Old **Spitalfields**, near Liverpool Street, is a great place to spot up-and-coming talent, as fashion and accessory designers run many of the stalls. The market has an organic food section too. On Sunday, nearby cobbled **Columbia Road** is busy with stalls selling every type of cut flower and houseplant imaginable; this fashionable area is also dotted with independent boutiques selling hip fashions, homewares and gourmet organic produce.

With six heaving indoor and outdoor markets, **Camden** is the place to go for arts and crafts, furnishings and alternative fashion. In the west, iconic, colourful **Portobello Road** is renowned for its antiques but also sells fashions, food and bric-a-brac – Saturday morning is the best time to go.

Further south, the new Market Halls put Victoria on the foodie map in 2018, with three glorious floors of permanent stalls including Japanese noodle bar Koya Ko; Gopal's Corner, a spin-off from cult favourite Roti King; and Bunshop from the duo behind the Marksman pub in Hackney.

South of the river, trendy **Borough Market** is a foodie heaven, with stalls ranging from the Spanish Brindisa to the resolutely

British Ginger Pig and from Kappacasein (a cheese lover's heaven) to the health-conscious Total Organic Juice Bar and Elsey & Bent grocers. Vibrant **Brixton**, meanwhile, is home to a medley of markets featuring street food from around the world.

ENTERTAINMENT

Whether you are after theatre, opera, clubs or pubs, there is no shortage of entertainment in London.

THEATRE

London's theatrical history goes back to a playhouse opened at Shoreditch in 1576 by James Burbage, son of a carpenter and travelling player. Nowadays, London's theatres – staging comedies, musicals and dramas – are concentrated in the **West End**. To buy discounted same-day tickets for West End shows, visit the 'tkts' booth in Leicester Square (www.tkts.co.uk; Mon–Sat 10am–7pm, Sun 11am–4.30pm).

Other theatres include the **National Theatre** at the Southbank Centre (see page 52; tel: 020-7452 3000; www.nationaltheatre.org.uk), which stages innovative productions of the classics, some excellent modern pieces and the occasional rousing musical revival. The **Old Vic** (see page 53; tel: 0844-871 7628; www.oldvictheatre.com) specialises in revivals of the classics, while the nearby **Young Vic** (see page 53; tel: 020-7922 2922; www.youngvic.org) leans towards more recent, experimental theatre. Chelsea's **Royal Court Theatre** (Sloane Square; tel: 020-7565 5000; www.royalcourttheatre.com) is famous for cutting-edge drama, and the buzzy café downstairs is a lovely place for a bite to eat or a drink, whether you are watching a show or not. **Shakespeare's Globe** (see page 55; tel: 020-7401 9919; www.shakespearesglobe.com), on

Bankside, stages works by the Bard and his contemporaries. East along the river by Tower Bridge, the Bridge Theatre (tel: 033-3320 0051; www.bridgetheatre.co.uk), is the new venture from Nicholas Hytner and Nick Starr, of National Theatre fame.

In addition to the West End theatres there are dozens of fine suburban playhouses and multiple fringe venues, championing new, experimental works. In summer outdoor theatre is popular, too, in venues such as **Regent's Park** (tel: 0844-826 4242; www.openairtheatre.com).

Musical theatre continues to be enormously popular, and the quality is generally high. Some shows are fairly permanently based at their theatres, such as the longest-running musical in the West End, *Les Misérables* at the **Queen's Theatre** (51 Shaftesbury Avenue; tel: 0844-482 5151; www. lesmis.com), and Andrew Lloyd Webber's gothic masterpiece, *Phantom of the Opera* at **Her Majesty's Theatre** (Haymarket; tel: 0844-412 2707; www.thephantomoftheopera.com). Other shows and exports from Broadway, like *Mamma Mia!* at the **Novello Theatre** (Aldwych; tel: 0844-482 5115; www.mamma-mia.com) and *Wicked* at the **Apollo Victoria** (17 Wilton Road; tel: 0844-871 3001; www.wickedthemusical.co.uk), have also made their mark.

MUSIC, OPERA AND BALLET

Top concert venues include the **Royal Festival Hall** (see page 52; 020-7960 4200; www.southbankcentre.co.uk), with its improved acoustics, and the **Barbican** (see page 63; tel: 020-7638 8891; www.barbican.org.uk), home of the London Symphony Orchestra; the **Royal Albert Hall** (see page 69; 020-7589 8212; www.royalalberthall.com) hosts the summer BBC Promenade Concerts (the 'Proms'), while the **Wigmore Hall** (see page 49; tel: 020-7935 2141; www.wigmore-hall.

org.uk) does chamber recitals. Lunchtime concerts are held in churches including Westminster's **St John's**, **Smith Square** (tel: 020-7222 2168; www.sjss. org.uk) and **St Martin-in-the-Fields** (see page 27; tel: 020-7766 1100; www. smitf.org) and Piccadilly's **St James's** (see page 43; tel: 020-7381 0441; www.sjp.org.uk).

The London Coliseum

London's main venues for opera are Covent Garden's **Royal Opera House** (see page 37; tel: 020-7304 4000; www.roh.org.uk), where ballet is also performed, and the **Coliseum**, commonly called the **ENO** (tel: 020-7845 9300; www.eno.org), as it's the home of the English National Opera (performances in English), in St Martin's Lane. For modern dance, try the capital's leading venue, **Sadler's Wells Theatre** (see page 77; tel: 020-7863 8000; www.sadlerswells.com).

Jazz venues include **Ronnie Scott's** (47 Frith Street; tel: 020-7439 0747; www.ronniescotts.co.uk), **Jazz Café** (5 Parkway, Camden; tel: 020-7485 6834; www.thejazzcafelondon.com) and the **Pizza Express Jazz Club Soho** (10 Dean Street; tel: 020-7439 4962; www.pizzaexpresslive.com).

London is one of the best places to catch live music in any number of contemporary genres. The big-name venue is **The O2** (Peninsula Square, Greenwich; tel: 0844-856 0202; www. theo2.co.uk), a 23,000-capacity arena housed in the former

Heading out for a night on the town in Soho

Millennium Dome. Other popular venues include the Art Deco **02 Academy Brixton** (211 Stockwell Road) and the more intimate **02 Shepherd's Bush Empire** (Shepherd's Bush Green; for both venues tel: 0844-477 2000; www.academymusicgroup.com), or the **Roundhouse** (Chalk Farm Road, Camden; tel: 0844-482 8008; www.roundhouse.org.uk).

NIGHTLIFE

London is a great place to party, with hundreds of bars and clubs offering an eclectic range of music to a diverse clientele. Soho has long been central to London's mainstream nightlife, and still has plenty of great bars, though it is usually best to steer clear of Leicester Square. Try **Bar Soho** (23–25 Old Compton Street; www.barsoho.co.uk), a fun spot in the thick of the action; unpretentious, lively cocktail bar **Be at One** (17 Greek Street; www.beatone.co.uk), and Swift (12 Old Compton Street; www.barswift.com), a split-level cocktail bar with a buzzy crowd upstairs and a speakeasy-style lounge on the floor below. Cahoots (13 Kingly Street; www.cahoots-london.com) is a vintage-Tube-themed bar, complete with sandbags, classic signs and an old Tube carriage.

Shoreditch and Hoxton (near Old Street tube station) draw trendy crowds. At **Cargo** (83 Rivington Street; www.cargo-london.com), live bands, DJs and a great café vie for space; **93 Feet**

East (Truman Brewery, 150 Brick Lane; www.93feeteast.co.uk) has a relaxed vibe with music ranging from indie to hip-hop to retro; while **333 Mother** (333 Old Street; www.333oldstreet. com) is a Hoxton stalwart offering highly eclectic music.

The rich, royal, famous and upwardly mobile like to party in the exclusive clubs of Mayfair and Kensington. Polynesian-themed **Mahiki** (1 Dover Street; www.mahiki.com) and the theatrical Cirque le Soir (15–21 Ganton Street; www.cirquelesoir. com) are favourite haunts.

Camden is the place to go for indie and rock music, with gorgeous, if faded, **KOKO** (closed for refurbishment until spring 2020; 1a Camden High Street; www.koko.uk.com) and sweaty basement venue **The Underworld** (174 Camden High Street; www.theunderworldcamden.co.uk) leading the way.

Brixton has a range of partying options as diverse as the area itself, including the **Dogstar** (www.dogstarbrixton.com), a dance bar at 389 Coldharbour Lane.

Dotted across town, superclubs such as **Fabric** (77a Charterhouse Street, Farringdon; www.fabriclondon.com) and **Ministry of Sound** (103 Gaunt Street, Elephant and Castle; www.ministryofsound.com) attract top international DJs.

For the LGBTQ scene, Soho and Vauxhall are your best bet, with endless bars and diverse clubs ranging from **Heaven** (The Arches, Villiers Street, Charing Cross; www.heaven-live. co.uk), home to the legendary G-A-Y club nights, to **Fire** (South Lambeth Road, Vauxhall; www.firelondon.net), serving up house and electro beats with plenty of flesh on show.

Most clubs don't get going until midnight; some run all night. The Night Tube has made getting home easier for clubbers, although this only runs on Fridays and Saturday nights. On other days, your only options are an expensive taxi or a night bus.

Taking a dip on Hampstead Heath

SPORTS

Londoners have always been a sporty breed. For those looking to stretch their legs, there is horse riding and boating in Hyde Park, swimming at Hampstead Heath and rowing on the Thames. Many of London's parks offer public tennis courts.

The **football** season runs from August to May, with matches usually held on Saturday and Sunday afternoons. The top London clubs are: Arsenal (Emirates Stadium; tel: 020-7619 5003; www.arsenal.com), Chelsea (Stamford Bridge; tel: 020-7958 2190; www.chelseafc.com) and Tottenham Hotspur (White Hart Lane; tel: 0844-499 5000; www.tottenhamhotspur. com). Wembley Stadium (tel: 0844-980 8001; www.wembleystadium.com) hosts the FA Cup final and national games, as well as concerts. **Rugby** is played from September to April/May. Major Rugby Union games are played at Twickenham (tel: 020-8892 8877; www.englandrugby.com/twickenham). **Cricket** is played in summer at the Oval (Kennington, SE11; tel: 0844-375 1845; www. kiaoval.com) and Lord's (St John's Wood, NW8; tel: 020-7616 8500; www.lords.org). Buy tickets well in advance for Test Matches.

Wimbledon is the venue for the famous two-week annual tennis championship in June/July. Seats for Centre Court and Courts 1 and 2 should be reserved six months in advance. However, you can queue on the day for outside court tickets, and you may be able to buy cheap returns in the afternoon. For information contact the All England Tennis Club (tel: 020-8944 1066; www.wimbledon.com).

One of London's most famous sporting events is the Easter **University Boat Race**, during which rowers from Oxford and Cambridge universities race along the Thames from Putney to Mortlake. The **London Marathon** in April attracts the top athletes from around the world, as well as roughly 35,000 other runners, many in outlandish costumes for charity.

CHILDREN

London's parks and attractions guarantee youngsters a fun time. The Diana, Princess of Wales' Playground, in Kensington Gardens, has a huge wooden pirate ship and wonderful Peter Pan-inspired playground. In nearby Hyde Park is the Diana, Princess of Wales' Memorial Fountain, where kids can dip their toes in. Animal-loving

☉ 2012 OLYMPICS

In July 2005, London surprised itself by winning its bid to host the 2012 Olympic Games. Considered a great success, the games saw long-neglected parts of east London transformed to house the main stadia and Olympic Village. The Olympic Park, now called the Queen Elizabeth Olympic Park, was set amidst newly created parkland in Stratford and included the Olympic Stadium, Aquatics Centre, Velopark and Basketball Arena. Various other events took place around London, including beach volleyball at Horse Guards Parade, equestrian events in Greenwich Park, gymnastics in the O2 Arena, football at Wembley, tennis at Wimbledon and open-water swimming in the Serpentine in Hyde Park.

The Tower of London

kids will enjoy a visit to **London Zoo** (see page 48) or the **Sea Life London Aquarium** (see page 51; look out for 2-for-1 offers with train tickets), while celebrity-spotters should visit **Madame Tussauds** (see page 49).

Children can clamber over the old buses and trams and play on pretend vehicles at the **London Transport Museum** (see page 38), while the **Natural History Museum** (see page 71) is home to the ever-popular robotic T-Rex. The **Science Museum** (see page 72) has the interactive Garden play space in the basement plus the Fly Zone with simulators. The **Tower of London** (see page 65) enlivens history thanks to Beefeaters with traditional costumes and stories to tell.

London has two toy museums. The **V&A Museum of Childhood** (Cambridge Heath Road; www.vam.ac.uk/moc; daily 10am–5.45pm; free) in **Bethnal Green** is the largest public collection of dolls' houses, games and puppets on view in the world and has plenty of space for little children to roam. On a smaller scale is Fitzrovia's **Pollock's Toy Museum** (Scala Street; www.pollock-stoys.com; Mon–Sat 10am–5pm, last admission at 4.30pm).

For toys to take home as gifts, shop at the vast **Hamleys** in Regent Street. **Harrods** is also fun for children. A ride on the **London Eye** (see page 51) is an exciting half an hour for older children.

CALENDAR OF EVENTS

January New Year's Day: London parade.

February Chinese New Year: celebrations in Soho's Chinatown and Trafalgar Square, including traditional lion dances and a parade.

March/April Oxford versus Cambridge University Boat Race: the mighty institutions battle it out on the Thames from Putney to Mortlake.

April London Marathon (second or third Sun): the world's largest marathon, with over 30,000 runners raising huge sums for charity.

May Chelsea Flower Show (third or fourth week): the most prestigious annual gardening exhibition in the world.

June Royal Ascot Races: horse races where the upper classes show off their new hats. Trooping the Colour (Sat nearest June 11): the Queen inspects the troops at her official birthday parade. All England Lawn Tennis Championships (late June/early July): the world's greatest tennis players compete for the Wimbledon title.

July–September Henry Wood Promenade Concerts, known as the 'Proms': classical concerts for eight weeks at the Royal Albert Hall.

August Notting Hill Carnival (bank holiday weekend): huge Caribbean street party around Ladbroke Grove and Portobello Road.

September Great River Race (Sat in early to mid-Sept): hundreds of traditional boats race from Docklands to Richmond.

October Trafalgar Day Parade (Sun nearest Oct 21): celebrates Lord Nelson's sea victory over Napoleon.

November State Opening of Parliament: watch the Queen and royal procession en route to re-open Parliament after the summer recess. Lord Mayor's Show (second Sat): a popular pageant of carnival floats and the newly elected Lord Mayor in procession from the Guildhall to the Law Courts. Guy Fawkes' Day (Nov 5): fireworks displays and bonfires across the city, commemorating the failed attempt to blow up Parliament. Christmas lights switched on in Oxford and Regent streets.

December Trafalgar Square is decorated with a huge Christmas tree, presented every year by the people of Oslo. New Year's Eve: spectacular fireworks display by the Thames.

EATING OUT

Although London's restaurants are expensive by many people's standards, reflecting the high cost of living here, eating out in the British capital has never been so good. The city has around 12,000 restaurants, covering every cuisine imaginable. At the top end of the range there are some world-class restaurants, charging commensurately high prices, some with multiple Michelin stars; at the lower end, there are places that offer very good value without compromising on the food. On the whole, London is also an excellent place to eat out as a vegetarian, with most restaurant menus featuring meat-free options and a recent swell of top vegan haunts reflects the rise of herbivores in the capital.

The main concentration of restaurants is in the West End, with the biggest variety in Soho. While many chain restaurants in Covent Garden offer good-value, pre-show suppers, the area has become an epicurean enclave in recent years. Upmarket Kensington, Chelsea and Notting Hill are home to numerous designer restaurants, while the City has many oyster bars and big-budget restaurants, aimed at the business luncher, and East London offers a combination of hip eateries across all budgets, serious foodie places and a concentration of ethnic restaurants.

THE REBIRTH OF BRITISH CUISINE

Not so long ago, British food had a very bad reputation. Lack of imagination, lack of taste and overcooked vegetables were often cited, and the cuisine was internationally derided, with the French President Jacques Chirac famously saying 'you can't trust people who cook as badly as that'. But how things have changed – the last few decades have seen a remarkable transformation in London's restaurant scene and a resurgence of interest in Britain's

indigenous cuisine. There is also an emphasis on high-quality locally sourced, organic ingredients, so one can now feast on Cromer crab, Cornish sprats, Gressingham duck, juicy Herdwick lamb or Galloway beef, served with seasonal organic vegetables.

The rebirth of British cuisine is largely due to a new generation of chefs, many of whom have achieved celebrity status. The outspoken chef Gordon Ramsay was one of the first of several London-based restaurateurs who raised expectations of what should be on offer, garnering Michelin stars along the way. Fortunately for those who wish to avoid forward planning (high-end restaurants often need reserving well in advance) and excessive bills, this culinary zeal has also filtered down to more modest restaurants and even the local pub. A major component of the city's social history, London has around 4,000 public houses. Several of these date from as long ago as the 17th century, and many retain the atmosphere of that era, with cosy decor and traditional oak-panelled walls. Many pubs concentrate on food as much as drinks, serving updated versions of traditional 'pub grub', such as bangers and mash, a Ploughman's lunch, steak and kidney pie and the traditional Sunday roast. 'Gastropubs' – light, airy, fashionably furnished bars that serve a more adventurous range of dishes – are found across the capital.

TRADITIONAL BRITISH FOOD

The somewhat nostalgic return to 'old-fashioned' food means that excellent versions of the following traditional British dishes are easier than ever to find.

Full English breakfast. This hearty meal consists of fried eggs, bacon, sausage, tomatoes, beans, mushrooms, black pudding and perhaps toast, all on one plate, served with a cup of tea or coffee. At traditional establishments kippers and porridge may also be on the menu.

Afternoon tea. This highly traditional and genteel event takes place in some of the grander hotels at around 3.30pm and consists of thinly cut sandwiches (often cucumber), scones with clotted cream and jam, a variety of cakes and a pot of tea. The brew varies from classic Indian teas such as Assam and Darjeeling to the more flowery Earl Grey. Venues include the Waldorf Hilton (Aldwych; tel: 020-7759 4091), the Ritz (see page 43), and the Dorchester (Park Lane; tel: 020-7629 8888).

Roast beef. The Sunday roast remains one of Britain's favourite dishes. At its best, succulent pink topside of beef is served

⊘ EATING AND DRINKING HOURS

In general, breakfast is served 7am–noon, lunch noon–3pm, afternoon tea 3–5pm, and dinner 6–11pm. In practice, you can eat whatever you want, whenever you want, if you know where to look – Soho and Covent Garden have the most options for round-the-clock dining. Although pubs can now apply for 24-hour licenses, most are only open Mon–Sat 11am–11pm (though many stay open a couple of hours later on Fri and Sat) and Sun noon–10.30pm. Many restaurants close on Sunday evenings, so it's wise to check beforehand.

together with Yorkshire pudding and a selection roast vegetables, accompanied by gravy and horseradish sauce or mustard.

Fish n chips. Good places to try this British staple are Rock & Sole Plaice (47 Endell St, Covent Garden), Sea Shell (49–51 Lisson Grove, Marylebone) and Geales (2 Farmer Street, Notting Hill).

Pie and mash. For a taste of the old East End look for a Pie and Mash Shop, such as Manze's (87 Tower Bridge Road). You'll get minced beef pie and mashed potatoes with a unique green sauce called liquor, made from parsley. Eels may also be on the menu.

Fish and chips

Puddings. Traditional English desserts are filling affairs, such as rib-sticking, steamed jam roly-poly or treacle (molasses) pudding. Slightly lighter are fruit pies and crumbles, with a top crust of crumbly pastry. Puddings are traditionally smothered in custard, a sweet, hot, vanilla-flavoured milky sauce.

INTERNATIONAL CUISINE

London's status as an international city attracts fine cooks from every part of the world. Over 50 major country styles are represented, from Afghan to Italian, Spanish, Turkish and Vietnamese. The top end is still dominated by French cuisine, though ethnic food is no longer just a cheap option – London has some of the finest Indian, Japanese and Chinese restaurants in the world.

WHAT TO DRINK

Traditionally, **beer** was to Britain what wine was to France. It comes in various forms, from lager (now the most popular form in Britain) to ale (brewed using only top-fermenting yeasts; sweeter and fuller bodied) to stout (creamy, almost coffee-like beer made from roasted malts or roast barley), of which the most famous brand is probably Guinness. Pubs generally serve beer either 'draught' or from the cask. In the case of the former, a keg is pressurised with carbon-dioxide gas, which drives the beer to the dispensing tap. For the latter, beer is pulled from the cask via a beer line with a hand pump at the bar. This method is generally used for what is often termed 'real ale': unfiltered and unpasteurised beer, which requires careful storage at the correct temperature. A slew of independent taprooms have opened in recent years, with many offering brewery tours and tastings.

The popularity of **wine** in Britain has increased dramatically in the last 25 years, and every pub or restaurant will have a wide selection available. English wines, especially whites, are becoming more popular, and can be found in specialist shops and farmers' markets, though you rarely see them on restaurant menus. Kent-produced Chapel Down is worth looking out for.

A longer-established English tipple is **cider**, produced predominantly in the Southwest since before the Romans arrived. Made from the fermented juice of apples, it is also known as 'scrumpy' (windfalls are 'scrumps'). The pear equivalent is called 'perry'. Fruit-flavoured cider is fashionable in some gastropubs.

Another speciality is **whisky**, produced in Scotland and Ireland. This is available as 'single malt' (malt whisky from a single distillery), as well as 'blended'. Most pubs in central London will offer a small selection of both, though aficionados may consider joining the Whisky Society, which has its tasting events at 19 Greville Street in Hatton Garden, Clerkenwell (www.smws.co.uk).

PLACES TO EAT

We have used the following symbols to give an idea of the price for a three-course meal for one, including wine and service:

££££	£55 and over
£££	£35–55
££	£25–35
£	below £25

WESTMINSTER

Cinnamon Club £££ *30–2 Great Smith Street, SW1, tel: 020-7222 2555,* www.cinnamonclub.com. It's more like a colonial club than the Old Westminster Library it once was. The haute cuisine take on Indian cooking is innovative and tasty, and the wines complement the spicy food well.

Gordon's Wine Bar ££ *47 Villiers Street, WC2, tel: 020-7930 1408,* www.gordonswinebar.com. Located just north of Embankment tube is this favourite London watering hole, where drinkers sit under the arches on chilly nights (though keep an eye on your bag) and out on the terrace in summer. Sherry and port are specialities here.

The Portrait ££ *National Portrait Gallery, St Martin's Place, WC2, tel: 020-7312 2490,* www.npg.org.uk/portraitrestaurant. When it comes to location, few can beat the National Portrait Gallery's top-floor restaurant with its wonderful views of Trafalgar Square, Big Ben and the London Eye. Above-average gallery food and a good-value pre-theatre menu (5.30–6.30pm), offering three courses for £25).

Rex Whistler Restaurant £££ *Tate Britain, Millbank, SW1, tel: 020-7887 8825,* www.tate.org.uk. Beautifully decorated with Rex Whistler's mural, *The Expedition in Pursuit of Rare Meats*, this fine restaurant in the basement of Tate Britain serves modern British food and has an excellent wine list.

SOHO AND CHINATOWN

Andrew Edmunds £££ *46 Lexington Street, W1, tel: 020-7437 5708*, www.andrewedmunds.com. A lack of signage out front gives a secretive feel to this cosy Soho hideaway. Inside, the wood-panelled walls are lit by candlelight. Dishes are simple but varied, ranging from rabbit to pasta.

Bar Italia £ *22 Frith Street, W1, tel: 020-7437 4520*, www.baritaliasoho.co.uk. Retaining its genuine 1950s feel, this is London's most famous Italian bar. No hype, just excellent coffee and a cosmopolitan crowd. Stays open through the night (closed 5–7am) and has a late licence.

Bocca di Lupo £££ *12 Archer Street, W1, tel: 020-7734 2223*, www.boccadilupo.com. Buzzy Italian restaurant serving a range of regional dishes such as risotto of Italian prawns and roast suckling pig.

Barrafina ££ *26 Dean Street, W1, tel: 020-7440 1456*, www.barrafina.co.uk. The same Michelin-starred Spanish tapas, the same marble-topped dining counter, the same snaking queue of hopeful diners – now just in a slightly bigger space on a different Soho street. Extensive list of Spanish wines; no reservations.

Dean Street Townhouse ££££ *69–71 Dean Street, W1, tel: 020-7434 1775*, www.deanstreettownhouse.com. The restaurant of this stylish Soho hotel manages to combine the style of a French brasserie with the delights of simple English food – the fish and chips are particularly good. The ambience is hip, and the service is attentive.

Mildreds ££ *45 Lexington Street, W1, tel: 020-7494 1634*, www.mildreds.co.uk. Imaginative vegetarian cooking served in retro, café-style surroundings. Vegan options are also available. Branches also in Camden, King's Cross and Dalston.

Randall & Aubin £££ *16 Brewer Street, W1, tel: 020-7287 4447*, www.randallandaubin.com. Named after the old delicatessen that inhabited this spot from 1904 to the late 1990s, Randall & Aubin is a buzzy, romantic place doing champagne, seafood and succulent roasts. Piles of lobster, crab and oysters greet you as you enter, the music is frenetic and the tables close to each other. Also does classic French and British dishes.

Spuntino ££ *61 Rupert Street, W1, no tel,* www.spuntino.co.uk. With no telephone, no reservations, a barely-there sign above the window and a self-consciously distressed interior, Brooklyn-style diner Spuntino could be accused of being a little too cool for its own good. But the small plates of American comfort food (mini sliders, truffled egg toast, mac 'n' cheese, pistachio cheesecake) are so tasty that you probably won't want to share them.

Xu £ *30 Rupert Street, W1, tel: 020-3319 8147,* www.xulondon.com. All dark wood panelling and silkscreen prints, this is a sleek place to try innovative Taiwanese classics like xian bing (pan-fried dumplings stuffed with minced pork), beef short rib pancakes and shou pa chicken (shredded meat topped with peppery skin).

COVENT GARDEN

L'Atelier de Joël Robuchon ££££ *13–15 West Street, WC2, tel: 020-7010 8600;* www.joelrobuchon.co.uk. French food with Spanish influences at this Michelin-starred restaurant. Foie gras, free-range quail, Scottish scallops, lobster and steak are just some of the offerings. Diners sit at a counter surrounding the kitchen so you can see the chefs at work.

The Barbary £££ *16 Neal's Yard, WC2, no tel,* www.thebarbary.co.uk. A horseshoe-shaped counter wraps around a small kitchen, where chefs rustle up north African-inspired dishes like octopus tentacle with pomegranate molasses and neck of pata negra pork. The naan e Barbari is divine, especially slathered in smoky baba ganoush. Expect a wait, or book online – there are only 24 seats.

Cork & Bottle £ *44–6 Cranbourn Street, WC2, tel: 020-7734 7807,* www.thecork andbottle.co.uk. An excellent retreat from Leicester Square, this casual basement wine bar offers decent food and a notable selection of wines.

Frenchie ££££ *16 Henrietta Street, WC2, tel: 020-7836 4422,* www.frenchie coventgarden.com. With only the letter 'F' marking its existence, this understated restaurant is just as chic inside. The daily-changing, French-influenced menu may include bacon scone with maple syrup and cream or Sussex pork with poached pear – portions are fairly small but surprisingly filling. The three-course set lunch menu is good value (£32).

The Ivy ££££ *1–5 West Street, WC2, tel: 020-7836 4751*, www.the-ivy.co.uk. If you succeed in getting a reservation at this, one of London's most famous haunts (reserve months, rather than days, ahead, although you may have more luck at lunchtime), you'll enjoy a surprisingly unaffected atmosphere, friendly service, a familiar menu (predominantly English with international favourites), a strong wine list – and some surreptitious star-spotting.

Rules £££ *35 Maiden Lane, WC2, tel: 020-7836 5314*, www.rules.co.uk. London's oldest restaurant (est. 1798), Rules has a traditional menu and beautifully decorated, old-fashioned dining room with wood panelling and Art Nouveau stained glass. The robust food is very English, with beef from Rules' own estate in the Pennines plus lamb and a variety of game.

Sarastro £££ *126 Drury Lane, WC2, tel: 020-7836 0101*, www.sarastro-restaurant.com. This restaurant makes for unusual dining with its extraordinary lavish decor and live entertainment (from pop to strings, to opera). The house slogan is 'the show after the show'. The food is rather more straightforward, although it has a Turkish slant. Value lunch/pre-matinée menus.

MAYFAIR AND ST JAMES'S

L'Autre ££ *5b Shepherd Street, W1, tel: 020-7499 4680*. Tucked away in the heart of Shepherd Market (see page 44), this quaint half-timbered restaurant offers an odd combination of Polish and Mexican food that works surprisingly well. Romantic atmosphere.

Benares £££ *12a Berkeley Square House, Berkeley Square, W1, tel: 020-7629 8886*, www.benaresrestaurant.com. Atul Kochhar's Benares is one of the few Indian restaurants in Europe to win a Michelin star. Dishes include smoked tandoori lamb cutlets, rogan jus and Kashmiri chilli turnips. Reservations essential.

Bentley's Oyster Bar & Grill £££ *11–15 Swallow Street, W1, tel: 020-7734 4756, www.bentleys.org.* With 100-plus years under its belt – the past 10 under the helm of chef Richard Corrigan – this Mayfair icon is synonymous with oysters (freshly shucked or creatively cooked), although its other seafood, fish and steak dishes are just as impressive.

The Diamond Jubilee Tea Salon ££ *4th floor, Fortnum and Mason, 181 Piccadilly, W1, tel: 020-7734 8040, www.fortnumandmason.com.* Opened by the Queen in her Jubilee year, 2012, this attractive restaurant is one of the best, and most expensive, places to have a proper afternoon tea. More than just cucumber sandwiches and cake, here you can sample smoked salmon and coronation chicken finger sandwiches and a wide range of patisserie.

Le Gavroche ££££ *43 Upper Brook Street, W1, tel: 020-7408 0881, www. le-gavroche.co.uk.* Consistently regarded as one of England's top restaurants, and holder of two Michelin stars. The food is a light, modern take on classic French cuisine.

Veeraswamy ££££ *Victory House, 99–101 Regent St, W1, tel: 020-7734 1401, www.veeraswamy.com.* London's oldest Indian restaurant is brought up-to-date with an adventurous menu combining North and South Indian cooking.

The Wolseley £££ *160 Piccadilly, W1, tel: 020-7499 6996; www.thewolseley.com.* Always busy, always glamorous, The Wolseley is the place to come for breakfast, afternoon tea and pre-theatre light meals as well as lunch or dinner.

BLOOMSBURY AND MARYLEBONE

Berners Tavern £££ *10 Berners Street, W1, tel: 020-7908 7979, www.bernerstavern.com.* Michelin-starred chef Jason Atherton is the man behind the menu at Berners Tavern, the painting-adorned restaurant of the London Edition hotel. The seasonal menu may include rack of Herdwick lamb or roasted Dover sole. Try the set lunch menu for three courses under £30.

The Gilbert Scott £££ *St Pancras Hotel, Euston Road, NW1, tel: 020-7278 3888, www.thegilbertscott.co.uk.* An elegant bar and brasserie run by

Marcus Wareing in a spectacular gothic setting. Named in honour of the original architect, the building is magnificent, and the menu celebrates traditional British dishes such as roast saddle of lamb, Angus fillet of beef, roast halibut and Yorkshire rhubarb.

Hoppers £ *77 Wigmore Street, W1, tel: 020-3319 8110,* www.hopperslon-don.com. The younger sister to Hoppers Soho, the Marylebone outpost of this popular Sri Lankan haunt offers the same delicious egg hopper (fermented-rice and coconut milk pancake) – but also the chance to book ahead. Aside from its namesake speciality, the menu also includes a range of roti, dosa and Tamil-style curries.

Locanda Locatelli ££££ *8 Seymour Street, W1, tel: 020-7935 9088,* www. locandalocatelli.com. Tucked away off Regent Street in the Hyatt Regency hotel is this Michelin-starred restaurant, where Giorgio Locatelli conjures up magical Italian dishes.

Orrery ££££ *55 Marylebone High Street, W1, tel: 020-7616 8000,* www.orre-ry-restaurant.co.uk. This beautiful dining room with Art Deco lines above the Marylebone Conran Shop is a mecca for foodies; if cost is an issue try the set menus. Stunning, intensely flavoured mains, prize-winning cheese trolley, memorable soufflés and a definitive wine list. Rooftop terrace too.

Oscar Bar and Restaurant £££ *Charlotte Street Hotel, 15–17 Charlotte Street, W1, tel: 020-7980 1007,* www.firmdalehotels.com. Behind an elegant façade of Georgian townhouses is the Charlotte Street Hotel, whose ground-floor restaurant is a busy, vibrant place, with walls brightly painted with scenes of 21st-century London. A great breakfast spot, but also popular for lunch with media types.

Pied a Terre ££££ *34 Charlotte Street, W1, tel: 020-7636 1178,* www. pied-a-terre.co.uk. Two-Michelin-starred cuisine offering dishes such as suckling pig served with turnips, chorizo and tarragon. Vegetarian tasting menu too, and set lunch (from £33 for two courses) is a bargain.

Rasa W1 ££ *6 Dering Street, W1, tel: 020-7629 1346,* www.rasarestau-rants.com. Easily recognisable by its signature bubblegum-pink frontage, the flagship branch in the Rasa chain of Indian restaurants produces quality, spicy Keralan seafood and vegetarian dishes. There is another branch (the original) at 55 Stoke Newington Church Street, N16.

Salt Yard ££ *54 Goodge Street, W1, tel: 020-7637 0657,* www.saltyard. co.uk. Tapas restaurant inspired by the flavours of Spain and Italy, with inventive options such as courgette flowers stuffed with goats' cheese. Charcuterie and bar snacks available too.

THE SOUTH BANK

Butlers Wharf Chop House £££ *Butlers Wharf Building, 36e Shad Thames, SE1, tel: 0207-7403 3403,* www.chophouse-restaurant.co.uk. Carnivores should go straight for the steak and kidney pudding, served with oysters, or pork chop and apple sauce. There are fish dishes for non-meat eaters.

fish! £££ *Cathedral Street, SE1, tel: 020-7407 3803,* www.fishkitchen.com. Located in the shadow of Southwark Cathedral – much to the annoyance of the clergy there – this all-glass restaurant serves a great range of fresh and simple dishes. Great fish and chips from here and the takeaway kiosk just outside.

Mesón Don Felipe ££ *53 The Cut, SE1, tel: 020-7928 3237,* www.meson donfelipe.com. Londoners in the know flock to this excellent tapas bar. Tables fill up fast, but there's often room at the bar. A guitarist performs from a raised alcove.

Oblix ££££ *Level 32, The Shard, 31 St Thomas Street, SE1, tel: 020-7268 6700,* www.oblixrestaurant.com. There are several upscale restaurants inside The Shard, all in the eye-wateringly expensive category (although dining in the building will save you the tower's £32 entrance fee). This 32nd-floor one, from German restaurateur Rainer Becker (of Zuma and Roka fame), offers spectacular views and New York Grill-style food. For a cheaper alternative, go for an express breakfast (£9 for juice, coffee or tea and pastries) or a set lunch (£34 for three courses) at the Aqua Shard (tel: 020-3011 1256; www. aquashard.co.uk), a contemporary British restaurant, on level 31.

Oxo Tower ££££ *Oxo Tower Wharf, Barge House St, SE1, tel: 020-7803 3888*, www.oxotower.co.uk. Some find it overpriced (the set lunch is a cheaper option), but this iconic spot is still hugely popular. The biggest draw is the fabulous view of the Thames through huge windows.

Le Pont de la Tour ££££ *Butlers Wharf Building, 36d Shad Thames, SE1, tel: 020-7403 8403*, www.lepontdelatour.co.uk. Butlers Wharf is Terence Conran land, *par excellence*, and the chic Pont de la Tour restaurant does fine French food such as *sole meunière* and glazed duck confit. The less formal Bar & Grill downstairs has a Thameside terrace and specialises in seafood.

Tapas Brindisa ££ *18–20 Southwark Street, SE1, tel: 020-7357 8880*, www.brindisa.com. Connected to one of the most popular stalls in Borough market, this restaurant is usually packed. Authentic tapas and a buzzing ambience. Some outside tables. No reservations taken. Also a branch near South Kensington tube.

The Anchor and Hope ££ *36 The Cut, SE1, tel: 020-7928 9898*, www.anchorandhopepub.co.uk. Meat and offal feature strongly on the menu of this popular gastropub. Reasonable prices, hefty portions and friendly staff. The no-booking policy can mean long queues, so arrive before the rush, if you can.

THE CITY AND EAST LONDON

Eagle ££ *159 Farringdon Road, EC1, tel: 020-7837 1353*, www.theeaglefarringdon.co.uk. This was the pub that launched a thousand gastropubs over 25 years ago with its pioneering menu of inventive dishes. The food has a Mediterranean bias and there is a good choice of European beers.

Hix Oyster and Chop House £££ *36–37 Greenhill Rents, off Cowcross Street, EC1, tel: 020-7017 1930*; www.hixoysterandchophouse.co.uk. Chef Mark Hix (formerly of The Ivy, Scott's and the Rivington Grill) showcases his modern British cooking. Dishes, which vary with the seasons, might include beef and oyster pie, Porterhouse steaks and grilled fish.

Luca £££ *88 St John Street, EC1, tel: 020-3859 3000*, www.luca.restaurant. A more laid-back – and affordable – Italian alternative to Michelin-starred sibling The Clove Club, located nearby in Shoreditch. Seasonal dishes may include grouse-filled ravioli or squid-ink bucatini with octopus. The three-course express set lunch is a bargain at £26.

Lyle's ££££ *56 Shoreditch High Street, E1, tel: 020-3011 5911, www. lyleslondon.com.* The first venture of chef James Lowe (of Noma and St John), Michelin-starred Lyle's is an airy, Scandi-style spot in a former tea factory. The four-course set menu varies, but its Modern British offerings may include white asparagus, fresh fish or Yorkshire game. There's a vegetarian menu and an a la carte lunch option too.

Madison Restaurant ££ *One New Change, EC4, tel: 020-3693 5160, www.madisonlondon.net.* In addition to upmarket stores, the One New Change shopping centre houses a cluster of bars and restaurants, including this one, which is impressively set on the rooftop, with great views of St Paul's. Open long hours it's as good for breakfast as for tapas and cocktails.

Moro £££ *34–6 Exmouth Market, EC1, tel: 020-7833 8336, www.moro. co.uk.* Located on the shabby-chic Exmouth Market, this laid-back restaurant serves Moorish cuisine, where lamb is charcoal grilled, tuna is wind-dried, lemon sole wood-roasted, and manzanilla sherry partners prawns and garlic. Tapas available all day.

Pizza East ££ *56 Shoreditch High Street, E1, tel: 020-7729 1888, www. pizzaeast.com.* Set in a former tea factory, this large industrial-chic restaurant is always packed thanks to its excellent market-fresh fare – pizzas, of course, but also meat and cheese deli boards and wood-fired mains including a super-rich pork belly. There is also a deli, where you can shop or just have a coffee.

St John Bread & Wine ££ *94–96 Commercial Street, E1, tel: 020-7251 0848, www.stjohngroup.uk.com.* Located opposite Spitalfields Market, this foodie favourite is celebrated for its 'nose-to-tail' eating. Fergus Henderson's kitchen offers simple, bold, often quirky dishes; for a bargain, go for breakfast (9–11am) and try the Gloucestershire Old Spot bacon butty. The more expensive sister restaurant, St John Bar & Restaurant, is a stone's throw from Smithfield's meat market (26 St John Street, EC1, same tel).

Smiths of Smithfield £££ *67–77 Charterhouse Street, EC1, tel: 020-7251 7950*, www.smithsofsmithfield.co.uk. Brunch on a Saturday or Sunday is really good fun in this vast post-industrial complex. Upstairs, a more refined experience is on offer in the restaurant along with views over Smithfield Market.

Tayyabs £ *83–9 Fieldgate Street, E1, tel: 020-7247 6400*, www.tayyabs. co.uk. There's frequently a queue outside this family-run Punjabi restaurant, and once you sample the mouth-watering authentic cuisine you'll understand why. The atmosphere is lively and the prices are low. The karahi lamb is a particular highlight. They don't sell alcohol, but diners are invited to bring their own.

The Cafe Below £ *St Mary le Bow, Cheapside, EC2, tel: 020-7329 0789*, www. cafebelow.co.uk. Situated in the atmospheric crypt of St Mary le Bow church is this excellent café/restaurant, offering a delicious range of breakfast and lunch dishes from Mon–Fri. Vegetarian choices always available.

Vinoteca ££ *7 St John Street, EC1, tel: 020-7253 8786*, www.vinoteca.co.uk. This fashionable little wine bar and shop is the original in a small chain (the other branches are in Marylebone's Seymour Place, King's Cross's King's Boulevard and Chiswick). It offers excellent, fresh, seasonal food in a daily-changing menu, with recommended wines by the glass.

KENSINGTON AND CHELSEA

Bluebird £££ *350 King's Road, SW3, tel: 020-7559 1000*, www.bluebird-restaurant.co.uk. The emphasis at this skylit restaurant, café and bar is on seasonal ingredients. It's a popular place for Sunday brunch, especially on sunny days when you can sit out in the courtyard. Downstairs is a posh food shop.

Claude Bosi at Bibendum ££££ *Michelin House, 81 Fulham Road, SW3, tel: 020-7581 5817*, www.bibendum.co.uk. After a 2017 revamp, Sir Terence

Conran's flagship restaurant returned with a new name, a new look and a new partner/chef – Claude Bosi of two-Michelin-starred Hibiscus. Thankfully, the beautiful stained-glass windows of the former French tyre company remain and the modern European cuisine is still faultless. There's a posh oyster bar downstairs if your budget isn't quite up to Bibendum.

Dinner by Heston Blumenthal ££££ *Mandarin Oriental Hyde Park, 66 Knightsbridge, SW1, tel: 020-7201 3833, www.dinnerbyheston.com.* Bespectacled scientist-superchef Heston Blumenthal (with head chef Ashley Palmer-Watts) works his usual eye-popping magic at his Michelin-starred London restaurant with experimental takes on historic British dishes from the 14th to the 19th centuries. The 'meat fruit' (chicken mousse fashioned like a fruit) is of particular note; his mains include such delights as spiced pigeon with ale and artichokes. For those on a more modest budget, the weekday set lunch costs £40 for three courses.

Fifth Floor, Harvey Nichols £££ *109–25 Knightsbridge, SW1, tel: 020-7235 5250, www.harveynichols.com.* This elegant restaurant at the top of the department store has an excellent reputation and is surprisingly child-friendly. Patisseries and puddings are made on the day, and starters and main courses are always enticing.

Hereford Road ££ *3 Hereford Road, Notting Hill Gate, W2, tel: 020-7727 1144, www.herefordroad.org.* Splendid British cooking enthusiastically served at this former butcher's. Try devilled lamb's kidneys, calf's brains and crispy pork with dandelion; followed by traditional desserts such as apple crumble.

Ottolenghi ££ *63 Ledbury Road, Notting Hill, W11, tel: 020-7727 1121, www.ottolenghi.co.uk. Also at 50 Artillery Lane, Spitalfields, E1, tel: 020-7247 1999.* Fabulous fresh food made on the premises – sit at the communal table or take away.

Vingt-Quatre ££ *325 Fulham Road, SW10, tel: 020-7376 7224, www.vq24hours.com.* As its name implies, this restaurant serves good hot meals 24 hours a day, with a licence to serve alcohol to match. It's particularly popular among the trendy, well-heeled Kensington locals.

A–Z TRAVEL TIPS

A SUMMARY OF PRACTICAL INFORMATION

A Accommodation 119

Airports 119

B Budgeting for
Your Trip 121

C Climate 122

Clothing 122

Crime and Safety 122

D Driving 122

E Electricity 123

Embassies and
Consulates 124

Emergencies 124

G Getting to London 124

Guided Tours 125

H Health and Medical
Care 126

L LGBTQ Travellers 127

M Maps 127

Media 127

Money 127

O Opening Hours 128

P Police 128

Post Offices 128

Public Holidays 128

T Telephones 129

Time Zones 129

Tipping 129

Toilets 129

Tourist Information 130

Transport 130

Travellers with
Disabilities 132

V Visas and Entry
Requirements 133

W Websites and Internet
Access 133

A

ACCOMMODATION

London has a wide range of accommodation, but bargains are hard to come by, as are affordable hotels right in the centre of the city. It's important to book ahead, as London fills up in the summer, but if you arrive without a reservation, head for a Tourist Information Centre (see page 130) or search Visit London's accommodation booking service at www.visitlondon.com.

AIRPORTS

London is served by five airports: the two major hubs are Heathrow and Gatwick, while Stansted, Luton (both north of the centre) and London City are primarily for chartered, budget or short-haul flights.

Heathrow (tel: 0844-335 1801; www.heathrow.com) is 15 miles (24km) west of central London. The fastest connection from the airport to central London is the Heathrow Express (www.heathrowexpress.com) to Paddington Station, which takes 15 minutes and runs every 15 minutes between 5.10am and 11.25pm. The fare is a hefty £25 single at peak times (£22 off-peak) and 37 return. Heathrow Connect (www.heathrowconnect.com) runs a cheaper service that takes 25 minutes and costs £10.30. There is also a direct Underground route (£6 single), on the Piccadilly Line, which reaches the West End in around 50 minutes. It operates from just after 5am until 11.45pm daily (just before 11.30pm Sun) and all through the night on Fridays and Saturdays. National Express (tel: 0871-781 8178; www.nationalexpress.com) runs coaches from Heathrow to Victoria Coach Station; the journey takes between 45 and 80 minutes, depending on traffic, and the single fare is from £6. The bus station is at Terminals 1, 2 and 3; from Terminals 4 and 5 take the free Heathrow Connect train to the bus station.

Heathrow is well-served by taxis; a ride in a London 'black cab' into town will cost £45–85 plus tip, and take 30–60 minutes, depending on traffic.

Gatwick (tel: 0844-892 0322; www.gatwickairport.com) is 27 miles (43km) south of London. The airport isn't on the Underground network, but the Gatwick Express (tel: 0845-850 1530; www.gatwick-express.com) runs every 15 minutes from London Victoria Station from 5am–10.44pm, and to Victoria from Gatwick from 5.59am–11.11pm. The train takes 30 minutes and costs £19.90 one-way (slightly cheaper online). Southern also runs services from Gatwick to Victoria, a journey time of 30 minutes (£16.70 one way). Thameslink trains run direct services from Gatwick to Blackfriars, City Thameslink, Farringdon and St Pancras International, with an average journey time of 30 minutes (from £19.40 one way).

easyBus (www.easybus.com) run services from Gatwick to West London while National Express bus services (tel: 0871-781 8181) operate the 32-mile (51km) journey between Heathrow and Gatwick (£20 single), taking between 60 and 90 minutes.

A black cab will cost around £80.

Stansted (tel: 0844-335 1803; www.stanstedairport.com) is located 34 miles (54km) northeast of London. The Stansted Express (tel: 0345-748 4950; www.stanstedexpress.com) leaves for Liverpool Street station every 15 minutes from 5.30am until 0.30am and from Liverpool Street to Stansted between 3.40am (Mon, Fri and Sat), 4.10am (Sun) or 4.40am (Tue–Thu) and 11.25pm, and costs £19 one way (cheaper if booked online); the journey takes around 45 minutes.

The National Express Coach (tel: 0871-781 8181; www.national-express.com) leaves for Victoria Station around every 15 minutes 24-hours a day, takes around 90 minutes and costs from £5 one way. There are also services to Southwark, Paddington and Waterloo.

The easyBus (www.easybus.com) runs every 15 minutes 24 hours a day, daily, between Stansted and London's Baker Street; single fares go from £6. Journey time is 1 hour 15 minutes.

Taxis cost around £80.

London City Airport (tel: 020-7646 0088; www.londoncityairport. com) is just 6 miles (10km) east of the City and is mainly used by business travellers. The airport has its own station on the Docklands Light Railway (DLR), which connects with the Underground network at Bank station.

Luton Airport (tel: 0158-240 5100; www.london-luton.co.uk) is linked by Thameslink rail services with London St Pancras International; some trains continue to Gatwick via Blackfriars. There is a shuttle bus between the airport and Luton train station. The journey to St Pancras takes about 45 minutes, and trains run every 10–15 minutes (hourly through the night). Green Line buses (route 757) run to Victoria in London, and take about 60 minutes (tel: 0344-801 7261; www.greenline.co.uk).

B

BUDGETING FOR YOUR TRIP

In general, London is a very expensive city, so make sure you come prepared.

Accommodation. Double room with a bath in Central London, excluding breakfast, including VAT: from around £110 to over £400 per night.

Meals and drinks. For a decent English breakfast, expect to pay anywhere from £9 and up, for a Continental breakfast £5 and up; for lunch (in a pub, including one drink) £8–12; for dinner (three courses, including wine, at a reasonable restaurant) £35–60. A bottle of house wine costs £15–25, a pint of beer £5; a coffee £2–3.

Entertainment. A ticket to the cinema will cost around £7–15; admission to a club: £5–20; and a good seat at a West End musical £50. Admission to many museums and art galleries is free, except for special exhibitions; others cost £4–16. Tickets for the most expensive attractions cost £16–35, but many are available '2 for the price of 1' if you travel by rail (see www.daysoutguide.co.uk).

Transport. A one-day, peak Travelcard (zones 1 and 2): £12.70.

C

CLIMATE

The weather in the capital is generally mild compared with the rest of the country. Good weather is certainly not guaranteed in summer, although occasionally the temperature soars.

CLOTHING

London is best approached with layers of clothing. While the city's reputation for rain may be somewhat exaggerated, you should pack an umbrella just in case. Fairly casual clothes are acceptable everywhere but classier restaurants and some nightclubs.

CRIME AND SAFETY

Serious crime is low for a city of this size, but the Dickensian tradition of pickpocketing is alive and well. Take the usual precautions. Use only black cabs and pre-booked minicabs. The threat of terrorism has led to an increase in police patrols, so don't hesitate to report any suspicious packages.

D

DRIVING

If you are only staying a short while in London, don't hire a car. Negotiating Central London by car is stressful for the uninitiated, due to the city's web of one-way streets, bad signposting and impatient drivers, not to mention expense due to the Congestion charge.

If a car is a necessity or you want to explore further afield, you should drive on the left and observe speed limits (police detection cameras are numerous). It is illegal to drink and drive, and penalties are severe. Drivers and passengers (back and front) are legally obliged wear seat belts. **Congestion charge/ULEZ.** Cars driving into a clearly marked Congestion Zone in inner London between 7am and 6pm Mon–Fri are filmed, and their owners are fined if a payment of £11.50 has not been made by midnight the same day. You can pay at many small shops, or by phone (tel: 0343-222 2222). See www.tfl.gov.uk for details. The Ultra Low Emission Zone (ULEZ) imposes an additional charge on vehicles which don't conform to certain emissions standards. See www.tfl.gov.uk for details.

Speed limits. Unless otherwise indicated these are: 30mph (50kmh) in urban areas (note that 20mph is increasingly common), 60mph (100kmh) on normal roads away from built-up areas, 70mph (112kmh) on motorways and dual carriageways.

Parking. This is a big problem in central London. Meters are slightly less expensive than multi-storey car parks, but only allow parking for a maximum of two or four hours; it can also be hard to find a free one. Many areas of central London operate 'pay by phone' parking only, for which you will need a credit card.

Breakdown. The following organisations operate 24-hour breakdown assistance: AA, tel: 0800-887 766; RAC, tel: 0800-828 282. The service is free to members only.

Car hire. To rent a car, you must be at least 21 years old and in possession of a valid driving licence (held for at least one year) and a credit card. The cost usually includes insurance and unlimited mileage but always check this.

All the hire major companies are represented in London; most have outlets at the airports as well as in the centre. Weekly rates start at around £150.

Alamo tel: 0800-028 2390; www.alamo.co.uk; **Avis** tel: 0808-284 0014, www.avis.co.uk; **Budget**, tel: 0808-284 4444; www.budget.co.uk; **Hertz** tel: 0843-309 3099, www.hertz.co.uk.

E

ELECTRICITY

The standard current in Britain is 230 volt, 50 cycle AC. Plugs have three pins rather than two, so bring an adaptor as necessary.

EMBASSIES AND CONSULATES

Australia: High Commission, Australia House, Strand, WC2B 4LA, tel: 020-7379 4334, www.uk.embassy.gov.au.

Canada: High Commission, Canada House, Trafalgar Square, SW1Y 5BJ, tel: 020-7004 6000, www.canadainternational.gc.ca.

Ireland: Embassy, 17 Grosvenor Place, SW1X 7HR, tel: 020-7235 2171, www.embassyofireland.co.uk.

New Zealand: High Commission, New Zealand House, 80 Haymarket, SW1Y 4TQ, tel: 020-7930 8422, www.nzembassy.com.

South Africa: High Commission, South Africa House, Trafalgar Square, WC2N 5DP, tel: 020-7451 7299, http://southafricahouseuk.com.

US: Embassy, 33 Nine Elms Lane, SW11 7US, tel: 020-7499 9000, https://uk.usembassy.gov.

EMERGENCIES

For police, fire brigade or ambulance dial **999** from any telephone (no payment required).

G

GETTING TO LONDON

By air. There are regular flights from most major airports in the world to London. For information on the city's airports, see page 119.

By rail. The Channel Tunnel provides Eurostar (tel: 0343-218 6186, www.eurostar.com) passenger services by rail from Paris Nord (2 hrs 15 mins), Lille Europe (1 hr 20 mins), Brussels Midi (2 hrs) and Amsterdam (3 hr 40 mins) to London St Pancras.

Vehicles are carried by trains through the tunnel from Folkestone in Kent to Calais in France by Eurotunnel (tel: 0844-335 3535; www.eurotunnel.com). The trip takes 35 minutes, and there are two to four departures every hour. Although bookings are not essential, they are advisable at peak times. Fares are cheaper late at night or in the early morning.

By ferry. Ferries operate between many British and Continental ports. Calais–Dover is the shortest crossing (75–90 minutes). Some of the main companies are:

Brittany Ferries, tel: 0330-159 7000 (UK), www.brittany-ferries.co.uk. Sails from Portsmouth to Caen, Cherbourg, Le Havre and St-Malo, Poole–Cherbourg and Plymouth–Roscoff.

DFDS Seaways, tel: 0871-574 7235 (UK), www.dfdsseaways.co.uk. Dover–Dunkirk and Dover–Calais.

P&O Ferries, tel: 0871-664 6464 (UK), www.poferries.com. Dover–Calais.

By coach. Eurolines (tel: 0871-781 8177; www.eurolines.co.uk) runs coaches to London from around 25 European countries. Within the country, National Express (tel: 0871-781 8181, www.nationalexpress.com) runs services from Victoria Coach Station on Buckingham Palace Road.

GUIDED TOURS

Bus tours. Hop-on hop-off double-decker bus tour operators include the Big Bus Tours (tel: 020-7808 6753; www.bigbustours.com) and the Original Tour (tel: 020-8877 1722, www.theoriginaltour.com). Departure points include Marble Arch, Trafalgar Square, Piccadilly, Victoria and Tower Hill.

Walking tours. London Walks (tel: 020-7624 3978; www.walks.com) offers almost 100 walks, many with literary and historical themes.

Black Taxi Tours. These offer a full commentary from knowledgeable cabbies. Tours are two hours long. Cost £150 per cab (£155 at weekends) – up to five passengers. For 24-hour booking, tel: 020-7935 9363, www.blacktaxitours.co.uk.

  River travel. Much of London's history is centred on the Thames, and seeing the city from the river provides a fascinating perspective. City Cruises (tel: 020-7740 0400; www.citycruises.com) serves the main piers down to Tower Pier and Greenwich; Thames River Services (tel: 020-7930 4097, www.thamesriverservices.co.uk) runs from Westminster Pier to Greenwich. Circular cruises between St Katharine's and Westminster Pier are available from **Crown River Cruises**, Blackfriars Pier (tel: 020-7936 2033; www.crownrivercruise.co.uk). MBNA Thames Clippers (www.thamesclippers.com) runs services from the London Eye to North Greenwich, with an additional weekday service from Putney to Canary Wharf.

Canal trips. Jason's Trip (www.jasons.co.uk) is a traditional painted narrow boat making 90-minute trips along the Regent's Canal between Little Venice and Camden Lock, Apr–Oct. The London Waterbus Company (tel: 020-3763 9981; www.londonwaterbus.com) runs from Camden Lock to Little Venice, with discounted tickets to the zoo at Regent's Park.

H

HEALTH AND MEDICAL CARE

EU citizens can receive free treatment on producing a European Health Insurance Card (EHIC). However, if the UK leaves the EU with no deal, EHIC cards will no longer be valid. Many other countries also have reciprocal arrangements for free treatment. However, most visitors will be liable for medical and dental treatment, so will have to pay for any non-emergency treatment. They should ensure they have adequate health insurance.

Major hospitals include Charing Cross Hospital (Fulham Palace Road, W6, tel: 020-3311 1234) and St Thomas's (Westminster Bridge Road, SE1, tel: 020-7188 7188). Guy's Hospital Dental Department is at St Thomas Street, SE1, tel: 020-7188 8006. For the nearest hospital or doctor's, ring NHS Direct, tel: 111.

Late pharmacies: Boots on Piccadilly Circus is open until 11pm Mon–Thu and until midnight Sat–Sun (closes 6pm Sun), while Bliss Chemist at 5 Marble Arch stays open daily until midnight.

L

LGBTQ TRAVELLERS

The LGBTQ scene in London centres around Soho and Vauxhall, with Old Compton Street in Soho offering specialist bars and shops. For information call the Lesbian and Gay Switchboard on tel: 0300-330 0630, www.switchboard.lgbt.

M

MAPS

The *London A–Z*, an invaluable streetplan of the city centre and suburbs, is available in a range of sizes from newsagents and bookshops.

MEDIA

London's *Evening Standard* (Mon–Fri; free and given out at rail and Tube stations) is good for cinema and theatre listings.

Listings magazines. Most comprehensive is the weekly *Time Out* magazine (free, handed out at Central London stations). The free paper *Metro*, also available daily in rail and tube stations, also has arts and events listings.

MONEY

Currency. The monetary unit is the pound sterling (£), divided into 100 pence (p). Banknotes: £5, £10, £20, £50. Coins: 1p, 2p, 5p, 10p, 20p, 50p, £1, £2. Many of London's large stores also accept euros.

Currency exchange. You will probably get the best rate by using an ATM, known as a cash machine, with your bankcard from home. Post offices and Marks & Spencer have *bureaux de change* that don't charge commission. At private *bureaux de change* (some open 24 hours), rates can be very low and commissions high.

Tax refunds. These enable visitors from outside the European Union to reclaim the 20 percent value-added tax when spending over a certain amount. Stores can supply VAT refund forms, which should be presented to Customs officials when leaving the country.

O

OPENING HOURS

Banks: Usually Mon–Fri 9.30am–5pm, although some close at 3.30pm. Saturday-morning banking is common in shopping areas.

Shops: Most open Mon–Sat 9am–10am and close around 5.30pm to 6pm. In commercial areas such as Oxford Street shops stay open until 8pm Mon–Sat (until 9 or 10pm on Thu). On Sundays major shops are only allowed six hours of trading between 10am and 6pm.

P

POLICE

Police, identifiable by their black uniforms and high-rise hats, are usually unarmed and, on the whole, friendly and helpful. For emergencies, tel: 999.

POST OFFICES

Most post offices open Mon–Fri 9am–5pm and Sat 9am–noon. London's main post office is at 24–8 William IV Street, near Trafalgar Square; it stays open until 6.30pm Mon–Fri, until 5.30pm Sat. The branch at 11 Lower Regent Street also opens Sun noon–4pm.

PUBLIC HOLIDAYS

On public (or 'bank') holidays, banks and offices close, but most other amenities remain open. They are: New Year's Day (January 1), Good Friday (March/April), Easter Monday (March/April), May Day (first Monday in May), Spring Bank Holiday (last Monday in May), Summer Bank Holiday (last Monday in August), Christmas Day and Boxing Day (December 25 and 26).

T

TELEPHONES

London's UK dialling code is 020. To call from abroad, dial the 44 international access code for Britain, then 20, then the eight-digit number. To phone abroad, dial 00 followed by the international code for the country you want, then the number: Australia (61); Ireland (353); US and Canada (1), etc.

With the ubiquity of mobiles (cell phones), London now has fewer public phone boxes. Those remaining accept coins and/or credit/debit cards. At coin-operated phone boxes, the smallest coin accepted is 20p; minimum call charge is 60p.

Useful numbers

Operator (for difficulties in getting through): 100

International Operator: 155

Directory Enquiries (UK): 118-500 or 118-888 or 118-118

International Directory Enquiries 118-505 or 118-811

TIME ZONES

In winter Great Britain is on Greenwich Mean Time. In summer (April–October) clocks are put forward one hour.

TIPPING

Many restaurants automatically add a 10–15 percent service charge to your bill. It is your right to deduct this if you are not happy with the service. It is usual to tip guides, porters and cabbies about 10 percent.

TOILETS

There are usually public conveniences in railway stations (often with a charge of between 20p and 50p), parks and museums. Few Underground stations have toilets for customer use (Piccadilly and the new Jubilee line stations are rare exceptions). Department stores often have free customer toilets.

TOURIST INFORMATION

The official tourist board maintains a website at www.visitlondon.com. It contains a huge amount of information on attractions, upcoming events and festivals, as well as practical information and a hotel booking service.

Personal enquires can be made at the **City of London Information Centre** (St. Paul's Churchyard, EC4M 8BX; tel: 020-7332 1456; www.visitlondon.com). The office is open Mon–Sat 9.30am–5.30pm and Sun 10am–4pm.

Another tourist information centre is located at the **Discover Greenwich Visitor Centre** in the Old Royal Naval College (Pepys House, 2 Cutty Sark Gardens, Greenwich SE10 9LW; tel: 0870-608 2000; www.visitgreenwich.org). The office is open daily 10am–5pm.

Travel and tourist information is also available at Euston, Liverpool Street, Paddington, Piccadilly, Kings Cross and Victoria stations.

TRANSPORT

For information on buses, underground, Overground, DLR and trains contact Transport for London (tel: 0343-222 1234; www.tfl.gov.uk). For national rail queries, tel: 0345-748 4950, www.nationalrail.co.uk. Both websites have excellent journey planners.

Oyster cards. These are smart cards that you charge up with however much you wish to pay, then touch in on yellow card readers at Tube and rail stations and on buses, so that an amount is deducted each time you use it. Oyster cards and contactless payment cards offer better value than buying single tickets, and travelcards valid for one, seven days, or one month, cover travel on all Tube, bus, DLR and local trains (within the specified zones).

Travel- and Oyster cards can be bought from Tube or DLR stations and newsagents. Visitors can order them in advance from www.visitbritainshop.com.

Children aged 11–15 travel free on buses with an Oyster photocard or can get half adult fare rate for up to 14 days with Young Visitor discount, if travelling with an Oyster or Visitor Oyster card-holding adult. Under-11s travel free on the Tube and DLR at off-peak times provided they are with an adult.

Underground. Known as the Tube, this is the quickest, though perhaps least rewarding, way to get across town. During the rush hours (8am–9.30am and 5–7pm) stations and trains are packed. Services run from 5am to around midnight and all through the night on Fridays and Saturdays on some lines. If you're heading for the end of a line, your last train may leave closer to 11pm. Most lines have trains every couple of minutes at peak times and every few minutes off peak.

Stations are split into nine zones, spreading out from the centre, and are charged accordingly (a single journey in zones 1–2 costs £4.90, but half the price with an Oyster card/contactless). A one-day Travelcard (also available on an Oyster card) offers unlimited use of buses, DLR, tubes and trains; a card for zones 1–4 is £13.10 peak. You can also buy seven-day, monthly and annual cards.

A Tube map can be found at the back of this guide. Some lines split into two, so always check the train's destination.

Docklands Light Railway (DLR). This is a fully automated railway that runs through redeveloped areas of east London and to Greenwich, and connects with the Tube network at Bank, Tower Gateway, Stratford and a few other stations. Tickets and fares are the same as for the Tube.

Buses. Most buses run fairly frequently from 6am–midnight or 12.30am and are then replaced by night buses (identified by an N before the number), which run every half hour or hour until dawn and usually pass through the Trafalgar Square area. Some buses run 24-hours a day. Cash is not accepted on board the bus network in London and paper tickets are no longer issued; touch in with an Oyster or contactless payment card as you board. The flat adult fare across London is £1.50.

In 2012 a new breed of double decker buses was introduced in London to modernise the fleet and replace the unpopular and problematic articulated 'bendy-buses' launched in 2002 by then mayor Ken Livingstone. Taking their inspiration from the classic double-decker

Routemaster, the New Bus for London (NB4L) was designed by Thomas Heatherwick, who designed the Olympic cauldron. The stylish driver-and-conductor buses feature an open back door and two sets of stairs. Around 1,000 of these Routemaster buses are in service.

Trains. London's principal National Rail stations are Charing Cross, Euston, King's Cross, Liverpool Street, London Bridge, Paddington, St Pancras International, Victoria and Waterloo. If you are staying in the suburbs, the fastest way into central London is often by this network, used heavily by commuters, but less packed than the Tube between rush hours.

Taxis. Official black cabs display the regulated charges on the meter. You can hail a cab in the street if the orange light on its roof is on, or you will find them at railway stations, airports and taxi ranks. You can book a taxi in advance at www.tfl.gov.uk (comments and complaints can be registered here too). Alternatively, book a cab or share a ride by using the smartphone apps mytaxi or Uber.

Licensed minicabs can only be booked via a registered office, either by telephone or online, so avoid any illegal ones touting for business on the street late at night. Addison Lee (tel: 020-7387 8888; www.addisonlee.com) is a good, licensed minicab firm. To receive the telephone numbers of the two nearest minicabs and one black cab number from TfL, text CAB to 60835 from your smartphone (charge).

TRAVELLERS WITH DISABILITIES

The definitive guidebook, *Access in London* by Gordon Couch, William Forrester and David McGaughey, is available to order via http://access-inlondon.org.

Information on accessibility of public transport can be found at www.tfl.gov.uk. The Visit London website (www.visitlondon.com) also has information about accessible hotels, attractions and entertainment venues. Inclusive London (www.inclusivelondon.com) and AccessAble (www.accessable.co.uk) are comprehensive online resources listing the access provisions and facilities for different sites, including hotels, shops, attractions and arts and entertainment venues.

V

VISAS AND ENTRY REQUIREMENTS

EU nationals will need their **passport** or **national ID card** to enter the UK. A **visa** to visit the United Kingdom is not required by nationals of member states of the European Economic Area (EEA), the Commonwealth (including Australia, Canada, New Zealand and South Africa, as long as the stay does not exceed three months) and the USA. Nationals of other countries (and for longer stays for those listed above) should check with the British Embassy and apply for a visa, if necessary, in good time. For up-to-date official information on visas, visit www.gov.uk/check-uk-visa

Customs. Free exchange of non-duty-free goods for personal use is allowed between countries within the EU, but with UK's imminent departure from the EU, limits and restrictions are likely to be imposed on goods.

W

WEBSITES AND INTERNET ACCESS

Websites that may interest visitors to London include:

www.visitlondon.com – London Tourist Board site

www.standard.co.uk – maintained by the *Evening Standard* newspaper, with detailed listings

http://streetsensation.co.uk – see which shops are on the city's favourite streets

www.tfl.gov.uk – travel information from Transport for London

www.bbc.co.uk – the BBC's vast site, with news, weather and listings

Internet cafés and Wifi access

London has internet cafés in practically all areas. Most hotels, cafés and public areas (including some railway stations) now have free Wifi.

RECOMMENDED HOTELS

There are hotels all over London, and while accommodation is generally fairly expensive for what you get, there is a growing number of new hotels offering affordable accommodation in a central location. Many of these belong to mid-range chains, in convenient areas such as the South Bank and the City.

In general, hotels in the West End and Mayfair tend to be expensive, with plenty of upmarket options but little choice at the lower end of the scale. The Bloomsbury/Marylebone area to the north is a clever option – it's central and characterful, but prices are more reasonable. There are some delightfully old-fashioned hotels in Victoria, and the streets close to the station are full of terraced bed-and-breakfast accommodation. There are also streets full of townhouse hotels in Kensington and Chelsea, offering dependable comfort in the middle-to-upper price bracket. Most hotels have free Wifi in the lobby areas.

The Youth Hostel Association (YHA; www.yha.org.uk) has six London hostels including the central 104 Bolsover Street, W1 (tel: 0845-371 9154) and 36–8 Carter Lane, near St Paul's (tel: 0845-371 9012). Beds from around £20/night. Independent hostel groups include St Christopher's (www.st-christophers.co.uk), which has eight hostels in London.

As a basic guide, the prices listed below are for a double room, not including breakfast. Short-term home rental companies like Airbnb (www.airbnb.co.uk) and HomeAway (www.homeaway.com) offer local, often relatively cheap accommodation in excellent locations.

££££	more than £300
£££	£200–300
££	£120–200
£	under £120

THE WEST END

Hazlitt's Hotel £££ *6 Frith Street, W1D 3JA, tel: 020-7434 1771, www. hazlittshotel.com.* Spread across four early 18th-century houses in the heart of Soho, elegant Hazlitt's (named after the great English literary critic) is packed with gorgeous antiques and full of character.

ME London £££ *336 The Strand, WC2R 1HA, tel: 020-7395 3400, www.melia.com/en*. This cutting-edge luxury hotel overlooks the Thames and has a rooftop restaurant and bar. The 157 inspired guestrooms include 16 suites and there is a 24-hour gym.

The Savoy ££££ *Strand, WC2R 0EU, tel: 020-7836 4343, www.fairmont.com/savoy*. This large London landmark, set back from the road, has a solid reputation for comfort, tradition and personal service. A massive £220m refurbishment has restored its reputation as one of London's very best hotels.

The Waldorf Hilton ££££ *Aldwych, WC2B 4DD, tel: 020-7836 2400, www.hilton.co.uk/waldorf*. Renowned Edwardian hotel with 298 rooms. Modernised and with a superb location, close to Covent Garden and Theatreland. Rooms come with plasma TVs and original Edwardian washstands. Restaurant, bar, gym, sauna and swimming pool all onsite.

MAYFAIR

Brown's Hotel ££££ *30 Albemarle Street, W1S 4BP, tel: 020-7493 6020, www.brownshotel.com*. A distinguished, very British, Victorian-style hotel with 115 rooms and 33 suites and an urban spa in a smart Mayfair location.

Claridge's ££££ *Brook Street, W1K 4HR, tel: 020-7629 8860, www.claridges.co.uk*. This London institution with splendid Art Deco reception has long had a reputation for dignity, graciousness and lack of pretension. Lovely central location. Health club and spa, plus a new fine-dining restaurant by renowned chef Daniel Humm and restaurateur Will Guidara, of Eleven Madison Park and NoMad fame.

Covent Garden Hotel ££££ *10 Monmouth Street, WC2H 9HB, tel: 020-7806 1000, www.firmdalehotels.com*. Understated and chic boutique hotel, popular with visiting film stars. As well as its 58 rooms styled with a contemporary English aesthetic, the hotel offers a luxurious film screening room, a DVD library, a gym and a beauty salon.

The Lanesborough ££££ *1 Lanesborough Place, SW1X 7TA, tel: 020-7259 5599, www.lanesborough.com.* Overlooking Hyde Park Corner, the stately neoclassical façade of the former St George's hospital conceals a refreshed look in keeping with its opulent Regency-style, along with a Michelin-starred restaurant and a luxury health club and spa.

The Mandrake £££ *20-21 Newman Street, W1T 1PG, tel: 020-3146 7770, www.themandrake.com.* Luxury Fitzrovia boutique hotel arranged around a central courtyard draped in jasmine and trailing plants. There's an inventive French restaurant, bar, theatre for film screenings and 34 theatrically designed rooms and suites, some with indoor terraces.

BLOOMSBURY AND MARYLEBONE

The Academy ££ *21 Gower Street, WC1E 6HG, tel: 020-7631 4115, www.theacademyhotel.co.uk.* This delightful boutique hotel is housed within five elegant Georgian townhouses and attempts to recreate for its guests life in 19th-century Bloomsbury (only with all mod cons). The 50 guest rooms are furnished in romantic style in keeping with the architecture, and there are lovely gardens where afternoon tea can be taken. Bar and dining room. No lift.

Grange Blooms Hotel ££ *7 Montague Street, WC1B 5BP, tel: 020-7323 1717, www.grangehotels.com.* Located very close to the British Museum in the heart of Bloomsbury, this elegant, traditional hotel in an 18th-century townhouse has 26 en-suite rooms decorated in traditional style, a pretty paved garden and breakfast room.

The Regency Hotel Westend £ *19 Nottingham Place, W1U 5LQ, tel: 020-7486 5347, www.regencyhotelwestend.co.uk.* An elegantly converted mansion with 20 comfortable rooms close to Regent, Oxford and Harley streets. No restaurant, just a breakfast room.

St Pancras Renaissance ££££ *Euston Road, NW1 2AR, tel: 020-7841 3540, www.marriott.co.uk.* Glorious Victorian-Gothic public areas at Sir George Gilbert Scott's restored Midland Grand hotel by St Pancras station. There are 245 rooms, including 38 suites with butler service.

Amenities include the Gilbert Scott brasserie run by Marcus Wareing, a Victorian-tiled pool and a spa.

The Zetter Townhouse Marylebone £££ *28–30 Seymour Street, W1H 7JB, tel: 020-7324 4577,* www.thezettertownhouse.com. The hotel equivalent of a cabinet of curiosities: quirky, intriguing and mesmerising. Inspired by Sir John Soane's museum, this stylishly eccentric 24-bedroom Georgian townhouse is peppered with playful swan sculptures, glass-fronted display cabinets and Chinoiserie peacocks. Cool cocktail lounge with clandestine vibe. Sister hotel in Clerkenwell.

THE SOUTH BANK

Mad Hatter ££ *3–7 Stamford Street, SE1 9NY, tel: 020-7401 9222,* www. madhatterhotel.co.uk. Thirty surprisingly stylishly designed rooms above a Fuller's pub in a good location just a short stroll from Tate Modern and the other attractions on the South Bank.

Sea Containers London ££ *20 Upper Ground, SE1 9PD, tel: 020-3747 1000,* www.seacontainers.com. On the banks of the Thames, the design of this bold and sleek hotel is inspired by 1920s cruise-ship glamour, incorporating contemporary twists; a giant, copper clad wall represents the hull of the ship. Newly independent since 2019, the 359-room hotel is still home to the Sea Containers restaurant, spa and Art Deco rooftop bar with outdoor terrace, plus the new Lyaness bar on the ground floor.

THE CITY

Andaz London Liverpool Street ££££ *40 Liverpool Street, EC2M 7QN, tel: 020-7961 1234,* www.hyatt.com. In the heart of the Square Mile, Andaz (formerly the Great Eastern Hotel) offers a different approach to guest services. The ethos is 'casual luxury'; instead of a reception desk, a member of staff will greet you and then look after you throughout your stay. The über-stylish contemporary decor should appeal to both corporate and creative types.

easyHotel £ *80 Old Street, EC1V 9AZ, tel: 084-3902 7000,* www.easyhotel. com. This frill-free 92-room Barbican hotel is clean, convenient and extremely well priced. The earlier you book, the cheaper the room. Other branches at Earl's Court, Heathrow, Paddington, South Kensington and Victoria; also in Luton, handy for London Luton Airport. Internet bookings only.

Fox & Anchor ££ *115 Charterhouse Street, Smithfield, EC1M 6AA, tel: 020-7250 1300*, www.foxandanchor.com. For a sense of the atmosphere of Victorian London, this immaculately restored pub near Smithfield market is a heritage attraction in itself. The six individually styled rooms combine modern comforts with period features, including roll-top baths, leaded windows, plush furnishings and luxury toiletries. The gastro-pub downstairs serves scrumptious British cuisine.

The Hoxton Hotel £ *81 Great Eastern Street, Old Street, EC2A 3HU, tel: 020-7550 1000*, www.thehoxton.com. An innovative hotel with an urban funky look, the Hoxton is well situated both for the City and for some of the capital's best nightlife. The well-designed rooms offer outstanding value and the latest in hipster chic.

Malmaison £££ *18-21 Charterhouse Square, Clerkenwell, EC1M 6AH, tel: 020-3750 9402*, www.malmaison.com. Located in a beautiful Victorian building on the edge of the City in the fashionable Clerkenwell district, the Malmaison has atmosphere and style without sky-high room rates. The 97 rooms are designed with stylish fabrics and smart bathrooms, and the brasserie and bar come highly recommended.

The Ned £££ *27 Poultry, EC2R 8AJ, tel: 020-3828 2000*, www.thened.com. The brainchild of Soho House founder Nick Jones, this 252-room hotel is set in the former Midland Bank HQ, within the City's Square Mile. Seven restaurants are spread across the grand banking hall and there's a basement bar set in the old bank vaults. There's a wellness centre, Cowshed spa and rooftop pool with views of St Paul's.

VICTORIA AND EARL'S COURT

Artist Residence ££ *52 Cambridge Street, SW1V 4QQ, tel: 020-3019 8610*, www.artistresidence.co.uk. Art-rich boutique within a 20-minute walk of

Tate Britain. Ten high-ceilinged rooms and suites (latter with claw-foot tubs) exude an artfully distressed vibe – upcycled headboards, tea-chest bedside tables, exposed brick. Lovely brasserie above a speakeasy-style basement cocktail bar. Great value.

The Nadler Kensington ££ *25 Courtfield Gardens, SW5 0PG, tel: 020-7244 2255,* www.thenadler.com. Taking the principles and style of boutique hotels to the budget market, this 4-star hotel offers 'studios' with their own fridges, microwaves and media facilities. Great for solo travellers or friends, with 'luxury bunk' options. Also other branches in Soho and next to Buckingham Palace.

The Rubens £££ *39–41 Buckingham Palace Road, SW1W 0PS, tel: 020-7834 6600,* www.rubenshotel.com. Traditional hotel with a smart location near the Royal Mews, but also conveniently close to Victoria station. Ten suites, 143 rooms, and eight 'royal' rooms that are themed around British monarchs.

KENSINGTON AND CHELSEA

Berkeley Hotel ££££ *Wilton Place, SW1X 7RL, tel: 020-7235 6000,* www.the-berkeley.co.uk. With its 2016 glass and steel show-stopping entrance, inside the hotel offers a country-house atmosphere, a health suite and rooftop pool. Among the restaurants is Marcus Wareing at The Berkeley, serving modern European cuisine.

Blakes Hotel £££ *33 Roland Gardens, SW7 3PF, tel: 020-7370 6701,* www.blakeshotels.com. Inspired by designer Anouska Hempel, this hotel's discreet exterior belies the splendid rooms, designed variously in romantic, grand and exotic styles. There is a lovely courtyard and restaurant too.

The Gore £££ *190 Queen's Gate, SW7 5EX, tel: 020-7584 6601,* www.gore-hotel.com. Idiosyncratic 50-room hotel on a quiet street close to the Royal Albert Hall. Every centimetre of the walls seems to be covered in paintings and prints, and the rooms are sumptuous. Popular with a lively, fashionable crowd. The excellent restaurant on the ground floor is perfect for pre-theatre dining.

INDEX

10 Downing Street 28
Albert Memorial 69
Anchor Inn 57
Apsley House Art Collection 68
Bank of England 64
Bankside Gallery 54
Banqueting House 28
Barbican 64, 94
Bethnal Green Museum of Childhood 100
BFI London IMAX Cinema 53
BFI Southbank 52
Big Ben 30
Borough 92
Borough Market 58
Brick Lane 80
British Library 48
British Museum 45
Buckingham Palace 40
Burlington Arcade 44
Butlers Wharf 61
Camden 78, 92
Canary Wharf 81
Cenotaph 29
Changing the Guard 41
Charing Cross Road 90
Chinatown 36
Churchill War Rooms 29
City Hall 60
Cleopatra's Needle 39
Clink Prison Museum 57
Columbia Road 92
County Hall 51
Courtauld Institute of Art Gallery 39
Covent Garden 36, 90
Crown Jewels 67
Cutty Sark 83
Dennis Severs' House 80

Dr Samuel Johnson's House 63
Dulwich Picture Gallery 85
Fortnum & Mason 43, 90
Freud Museum 79
Gabriel's Wharf 54
Golden Hinde 57
Green Park 41
Greenwich 82
Ham House 86
Hampstead 78
Hampton Court Palace 87
Harrods 75
Harvey Nichols 75
Hayward Gallery 52
Hendrix, Jimi 45
HMS Belfast 60
Holland Park 71
Horniman Museum 85
Horse Guards 28
Hyde Park Corner 68
Imperial War Museum 53
Institute of Contemporary Arts 42
Jermyn Street 90
Kensington Palace 70
Kenwood House 79
Kew 86
King's Road 75, 91
Leadenhall Market 65
Leicester Square 36
London Dungeon 51
London Eye 52
London Transport Museum 38
London Zoo 49
Lord's Cricket Ground 49
Madame Tussaud's 49
Millennium Bridge 56
Monument 66

Museum of London 64
Museum of London Docklands 81
National Gallery 26
National Maritime Museum 84
National Portrait Gallery 27
National Theatre 53, 93
Natural History Museum 72
Nelson's Column 25
New Bond Street 44, 90
O2 Arena 83
Old Bond Street 44, 90
Old Royal Naval College 84
Old Vic Theatre 53
Oxford Street 34, 90
Oxo Tower 54
Palace of Westminster 29
Piccadilly 43
Piccadilly Circus 32
Portobello Road Market 73
Primrose Hill 78
Queen Elizabeth Olympic Park 81
Queen's Gallery 40
Queen's House 85
Regent's Park 48
Regent Street 33, 90
Richmond Park 86
Ritz, the 43
Royal Academy of Arts 43
Royal Albert Hall 70, 94
Royal Courts of Justice 62
Royal Court Theatre 93
Royal Festival Hall 52, 94
Royal Observatory 84

Royal Opera House 37, 95
Sadler's Wells 78
Savile Row 44
Science Museum 72
Sea Life London
    Aquarium 51
Serpentine Gallery 69
Shakespeare's Globe
    56, 93
Shard, The 59
Sir John Soane's
    Museum 62

Sloane Square 75
Soho 34, 90
Somerset House 38
Southbank Centre 52
Southwark Cathedral 57
Spitalfields Market 79
St Martin-in-the-Fields
    27
St Pancras Station 47
St Paul's Cathedral 63
St Paul's Church 37
Tate Britain 31

Tate Modern 54
Tower Bridge 60
Tower of London 66
Trafalgar Square 25
Victoria & Albert
    Museum 73
Wallace Collection 50
Westminster Abbey 30
Westminster Cathedral
    31
Wigmore Hall 50, 94
Young Vic Theatre 53

INSIGHT ⊙ GUIDES **POCKET GUIDE**

LONDON

Second Edition 2019

Editor: Rachel Lawrence
Authors: Lesley Logan, Joanna Reeves
Head of DTP and Pre-Press: Rebeka Davies
Managing Editor: Carine Tracanelli
Picture Editor: Tom Smyth
Cartography Update: Carte
Update Production: Apa Digital
Photography Credits: Getty Images 1;
iStock 5MC, 7R, 30; Lisa Clarimont 15;
Lydia Evans/Apa Publications 4TC, 4MC,
4TL, 5T, 5M, 11, 24, 26, 28, 33, 42, 53, 55,
56, 62, 69, 76, 84, 87, 100, 105; Ming Tang-
Evans/Apa Publications 4ML, 5TC, 5MC,
5M, 7, 18, 35, 37, 39, 41, 45, 47, 48, 50, 58, 66,
71, 72, 74, 78, 80, 82, 88, 91, 92, 95, 96, 98;
Peter Smith/St Pauls Cathedral 64; Public
domain 16, 20; Shutterstock 6L, 6R, 12, 60;
Stefan Johnson 103
Cover Picture: Shutterstock

Distribution
UK, Ireland and Europe: Apa Publications
(UK) Ltd; sales@insightguides.com
United States and Canada: Ingram
Publisher Services; ips@ingramcontent.com
Australia and New Zealand: Woodslane;
info@woodslane.com.au
Southeast Asia: Apa Publications (SN) Pte;
singaporeoffice@insightguides.com
Worldwide: Apa Publications (UK) Ltd;
sales@insightguides.com

**Special Sales, Content Licensing
and CoPublishing**
Insight Guides can be purchased in bulk
quantities at discounted prices. We can
create special editions, personalised jackets
and corporate imprints tailored to your
needs. sales@insightguides.com;
www.insightguides.biz

All Rights Reserved
© 2019 Apa Digital (CH) AG and
Apa Publications (UK) Ltd

Printed in China by CTPS

Contact us
Every effort has been made to provide
accurate information in this publication,
but changes are inevitable. The publisher
cannot be responsible for any resulting loss,
inconvenience or injury. We would appreciate
it if readers would call our attention to any
errors or outdated information. We also
welcome your suggestions; please contact
us at: hello@insightguides.com
www.insightguides.com

Legend

- Bakerloo
- Central
- Circle
- District
- Hammersmith & City
- Jubilee
- Metropolitan
- Northern
- Piccadilly
- Victoria
- Waterloo & City
- DLR
- Emirates Air Line cable car (Special fares apply)
- London Overground
- TfL Rail
- London Trams
- District open at weekends and on some public holidays

- ○ Interchange stations
- ○─○ Under a 10 minute walk between stations
- Step-free from train to street
- Step-free from platform to street
- National Rail
- Riverboat services
- Victoria Coach Station
- Emirates Air Line cable car

† Services or access at these stations are subject to variation. To check before you travel, visit tfl.gov.uk/plan-a-journey

MAYOR OF LONDON

tfl.gov.uk

24 hour travel information
0343 222 1234*

*Service and network charges may apply. See tfl.gov.uk/terms for details

© Transport for London   Reg. user No. 18/S/3357/P   Improvement works ma

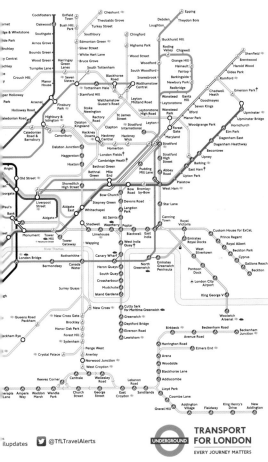

UNDERGROUND

TRANSPORT FOR LONDON

EVERY JOURNEY MATTERS

Plan & book your tailor-made trip created by local travel experts at
insightguides.com/holidays

STEP 1

Pick your dream destination and submit an enquiry.

STEP 2

Fill in a form, sharing your travel preferences with a local expert.

STEP 3

Receive a trip proposal, which you can amend until you are satisfied.

STEP 4

Book securely online. Pack your bags and enjoy your holiday!

DON'T MISS OUT
BOOK NOW AT
INSIGHTGUIDES.COM/HOLIDAYS